I0763153

***Ways of Listening* is a love letter to music, a sharp analysis of our current cultural reality, and a joyful celebration of the artists who keep creating against all odds.**

How has the internet changed the way we listen to, and love, the music that shapes our lives? Award-winning musician Rollie Pemberton (Cadence Weapon) interrogates our current musical landscape.

Music occupies a curious place in modern life, somehow omnipresent and disposable at the same time. Computers have democratized song creation. There is more music being produced now than at any point in human history, and streaming platforms are the ultimate distribution model for this vast bounty. But streaming relies on an algorithmic discovery system that guides the user's choices and encourages them to listen passively to the company's curation, while also dissuading the listener from searching for music and developing their own taste. Streamers offer meagre royalties to artists on their platforms, largely devaluing music in the public sphere. And social media companies have taught a whole generation of young listeners to perceive music as merely background noise for content.

This all adds up to a bleak landscape for the true fan, but there's another way. Pemberton delves deep into his own music discovery process to present a gentle reminder of another path for the contemporary music lover. He explores the obsession with the "mysterious artist" archetype, studies Charli xcx's groundbreaking *Brat* album rollout, assesses the magic of demo recordings, breaks down the Kendrick Lamar–Drake beef, and examines AI's struggle to understand italo disco's strange balance of classic and cringe.

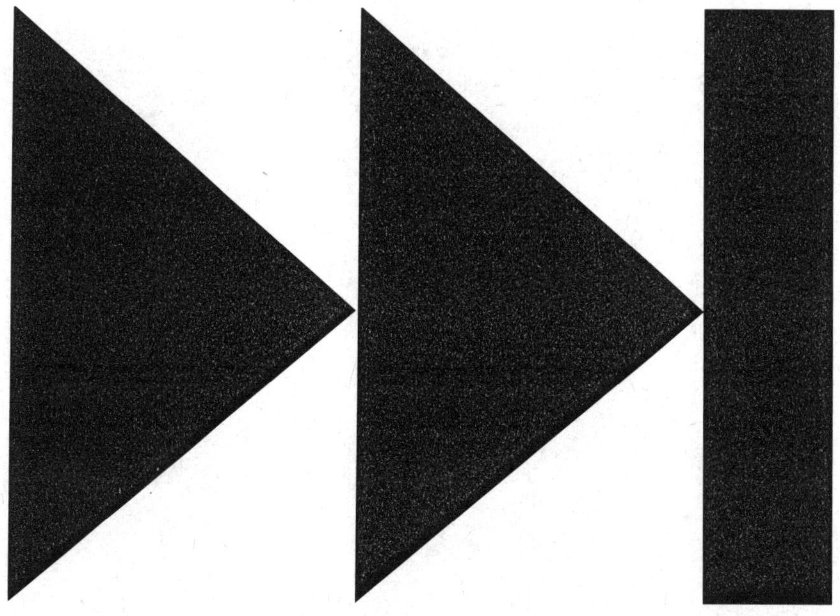

ROLLIE PEMBERTON

WAYS OF LISTENING

Building a Deeper Relationship with Music in the Streaming Era

McClelland & Stewart

Hardcover edition published 2026

The authorized representative in the EU for product safety and compliance is Penguin Random House Ireland, Morrison Chambers, 32 Nassau Street, Dublin D02 YH68, Ireland, https://eu-contact.penguin.ie

Library and Archives Canada Cataloguing in Publication

Title: Ways of listening : building a deeper relationship with music in the streaming era / Rollie Pemberton.
Names: Pemberton, Rollie, 1986- author.
Identifiers: Canadiana (print) 20250316625 | Canadiana (ebook) 20250316811 |
ISBN 9780771016042 (hardcover) | ISBN 9780771016080 (EPUB)
Subjects: LCSH: Music—Social aspects. | LCSH: Music and the Internet.
Classification: LCC ML3916 .P394 2026 | DDC 306.4/842—dc23

Cover design and art by Matthew Flute
Typeset in Granjon LT Std by Arthur Dennyson Hamdani
Printed in Canada

McClelland & Stewart
A division of Penguin Random House Canada
320 Front Street West, Suite 1400
Toronto, Ontario, M5V 3B6, Canada
penguinrandomhouse.ca

1 2 3 4 5 30 29 28 27 26

For Yari and Sara

Contents

Listen to the playlist as you read along:

https://cadenceweapon.substack.com/p/playlists

Introduction

When my memoir *Bedroom Rapper* came out in 2022, it was a relief to get my story on the page. Writing that book was about speaking my truth as a musician, sharing what it was like growing up Black in Alberta, and chasing my hip-hop dream against all odds. That aspect of *Bedroom Rapper* connected with the audience that I hoped it would: young aspiring musicians, people from the Prairies, and folks nostalgic for the early 2000s Canadian music scene. So much of the writing process for that book was about setting the record straight around my experiences working with my first label and management. Reliving all the ups and downs from the early years of my career was painful but cathartic.

What I didn't expect was how much readers responded to parts of the book that weren't specifically about my music career. I received so much positive feedback about the moments when I would zoom out and share brief histories of hip-hop, grime, and trap music; when I would wax poetic about obscure Canadian bands and Montréal's underground club culture. For those who primarily knew me as a musician, that side of the book was a pleasant surprise. So when it came time to decide what my next book would be, I felt a strong urge to dive back into music journalism.

The streaming era has completely redefined what it means to listen to music. Wading through today's oversaturated online landscape, we assess the numbers before we press play. Monetized social media has transformed music from a sacred communion with the spirits into the elevator music that you put behind your next reel. Music has been devalued by streaming platforms that have pushed artists to release more tracks at a faster rate, lest they be left behind by the algorithm. And music has been supercharged by new technology that allows you to create at the blink of an eye, but only if you're willing to exploit the existing works of other artists. It was these circumstances that encouraged me to write a guide to our present moment for those who might not be aware that a different way of listening is possible.

For as long as I can remember, I've been a human recommendation engine. I burned mix CDs for my classmates as a teenager and made suggestions to customers when I worked part-time at HMV in West Edmonton Mall. I reviewed rap albums for *Pitchfork* and started an mp3 blog out of my dorm room. I uploaded mixes via zip file to SendSpace so I could post them to my Facebook wall. I crafted detailed emails for my friend group with random albums I'd discovered that everyone needed to hear.

I've always had a desire to share music with others, and I've always done so with meaning and specificity. Getting close wasn't good enough. I tried to hit the bullseye on what people were looking for.

The app companies and streaming platforms feel no such responsibility. We entrust our music curation to companies that offer playlist placement to the highest bidder, that lack the expertise to properly define a genre's canon, that have a vested interest in keeping us on their app and make decisions about what to send our way accordingly. And as these platforms further insinuate themselves into our everyday lives, I worry that we might eventually lose our own skill of discernment by letting the machine make these choices for us.

I wrote *Ways of Listening* as a love letter to the more intentional and deeper way of listening to music that I grew up on, one that is slowly being forgotten. It's for the kids who never got the chance to experience a listening station, where you would rip open a CD, sit on a stool, and soak in an album. Throughout the book, I've highlighted some artists who have successfully navigated today's changing music landscape and broken down exactly what they've done to wrest back control from the system that musicians currently struggle against.

But it's also a book that looks to the future. If you're reading this years from now, I hope that it provides you with a retroactive glimpse of what it was like during a pivotal point for music culture. To listen on your own terms is a radical act in the streaming age, one that goes against lean-back listening, the algorithm, the stream farms, the exploitative apps, and the corporations that exist to profit from it all.

A Digger's Guide

Picture a record store in your mind. What do you see? Maybe there are flyers advertising local club nights on the wall. A person with a band t-shirt might be silently judging you from behind the counter. Music is undoubtedly playing, in your AirPods and from the overhead speakers. Sauntering around the shop, you might take a cursory glimpse at the new arrivals, lightly flipping your way through the racks. Your time spent in the store is probably brief. You ask about a particular release that you're looking for, make your way to it, and for most, that's where the journey ends.

For the diggers of the world, that's just the beginning. To us, different sections of the store seem to be glowing, as if the room were filled with items from a '90s point-and-click adventure game. We might actually start on the ground, beneath the record bins. That's where the dollar records and 12-inch singles are often kept, a treasure trove for those with abnormal levels of patience and dedication. We'll pull up a milk crate, sit down, and go to work. The real sickos go straight for the 45s, those 7-inch discs routinely ignored by most shoppers, despite being notorious for holding non-album cuts and rare samples and for playing at a louder volume and sounding better than LPs.

My digging instincts have turned me into the go-to person for everyone in my life when it comes to assessing and finding music. The parent of my kid's play gym pal asked me to help them discover some Kaytranada-adjacent tracks for when they jog around the neighbourhood. My old friends tapped me to provide the soundtrack for their wedding. The library in my hometown invited me to curate a selection of local artists for a compilation.

Digging for records runs in my family. My father, Teddy, was a radio DJ in Edmonton. I grew up around the library of music that he would play over the airwaves. He passed away when I was a teenager, and I have always been touched by how my mother, Michelle, has continued to take care of and add to the record collection that he left behind. As my concrete memories of him as a person fade over time, my concept of what a "Teddy record" is still remains. Those records are his legacy. They're all that we have left of him.

Ask me what I did two weeks ago, and I'll likely stare at you with a glazed expression. But if you looked through my record collection, you could easily chart out the path of my life: the trip to Barcelona where I found Li Garattoni's synth-jazz odyssey *Find Out What I'm Dreaming*, the rare copy of *Ebony Game* by Guy Cuevas that I snagged at a Toronto record show, or that time when I accidentally stumbled into Idle Moments in Bethnal Green and left with a copy of the Italian synth-pop group Radar's self-titled 1982 album, one of my most coveted grails.

Even the price stickers and markings on the record covers themselves tell a story, detailing each used record's individual journey as if they were stamps on a passport. DJs of the past marked their favourite tracks as well as the tempo of a song by hand on record sleeves before digital technology made that unnecessary. The messages etched into the runout grooves of records by mastering engineers are a secret language that can reveal the provenance and age of a particular pressing as if they were rings on a redwood.

At Kops Records on Danforth in Toronto, I picked up a promo copy of Ian Pooley's "Roller Skate Disco," and there was a highlighter-orange Virgin Music Canada press release from the '90s inside the sleeve urging DJs to play the single by comparing it to Daft Punk, Air, and the Chemical Brothers. I once bought a classic Detroit house record at Hello Records, flipped it over, and saw that it had a woman named Janice's phone number scribbled on the white record sleeve in red ink.

In 2016, my friend Roxanne drove me out to legendary Québec disc jockey Robert Ouimet's cottage in Roxton Pond, an hour and a half east of Montréal, so that I could interview him for a Red Bull Music Academy feature about Montréal's disco scene. Ouimet passed away in 2022, and on a recent trip to Montréal, digging at Death of Vinyl, I thumbed through some records that were stamped with "D.J. Robert Ouimet." I remember us passing by the friperies and casse-croûtes on our pilgrimage to meet this iconic figure who paved the way for Canadian club culture. Seeing his name on those records brought the memories flooding back.

In the digital music era, a slice-of-life moment like that no longer factors into the equation. It has become paramount that we take control of our listening habits in the algorithmic age. Music is a natural resource that the industry has tried to control and exploit in vain. Tech companies are desperate to unlock and monetize the secrets behind this art form that has rules and theory to govern it yet remains as unruly and wild as a gull cresting a sea squall. Music is a communion with the spirits, an ever-growing oral history that binds us together as human beings. It's important to remember that it's not just a product.

What we often gain from algorithmic recommendations is a shallow understanding of any given scene or genre. I can't count how many times I have looked at a Spotify-generated playlist for a specific genre and seen it populated with totally incorrect or irrelevant songs and artists. I worry about the impact this could have on young music lovers who might not go beyond absorbing what is served up to them by these apps. It feels like music's version of fake news, clickbait playlists designed for maximum streamability with no regard for how they might alter the perception of music history in a permanent and erroneous way.

Spotify has encouraged the homogenization of contemporary music by deprioritizing anything that could be considered challenging. TikTok has trained a generation of young people to think of music as a backdrop for content. So much of what now hits these platforms is designed to inspire uninterrupted, frictionless, passive listening. We risk a bland existence if we only accept recommendations that have a capacity for smoothness.

Many tout the broad spectrum of music available on streaming platforms as one of their primary benefits, but I believe that logic is somewhat flawed. When I DJ, some of the most floor-filling records in my crate are the ones that have never been found on the apps. Others exist in a quasi-legal grey area, composed of uncleared samples or released on defunct labels. Streamers and diggers are likely to hold drastically different perspectives on music history.

In Frank Broughton and Bill Brewster's now-antiquated 2003 guide *How to DJ Right: The Art and Science of Playing Records*, there's a short and still-timely section entitled "Luddite Lament" in which they bemoan the nascent emergence of digital music, worrying that we might start taking our sudden unlimited access for granted. "When everything is easy to find, can anything be rare or special?" they ask. "A vinyl collector might spend years on the trail of a rare record, all the time building up its importance and learning about its creator. By the time he finally owns it, he has the respect and understanding to go with it."

Music journalist Liz Pelly touches on Spotify's deleterious role in altering music's past, present, and future in her essential book *Mood Machine: The Rise of Spotify and the Costs of the Perfect Playlist*. The app's recommendation engine promotes "a weird data-refracted version of music culture" that is "a top-down version of culture branding itself as a bottom-up version of culture." Through its genre playlists, Spotify presents itself as an authority, perfectly comfortable with being perceived as the final word on the musical canon.

In the same way that we ascribe personal meaning to a mixtape made for us by a cherished friend, we reward Spotify with our loyalty and our dollars when it occasionally gets something right. But how would you feel if you learned that that same friend had taken money in exchange for getting a song placed on the mix that they made you? You'd likely lose trust in them after that, right? Spotify's Discovery Mode is just that—a payola-like marketing tool that allows artists and labels to make their songs more likely to be featured in algorithmic recommendations like Radio, Autoplay, and Mixes in exchange for a 30 percent commission on the streams generated by the placements.

This means that whenever a recommendation on Spotify is presented to us as if it is purely based on our listening habits and what the app thinks that we would personally like, there's a high probability that paid sponsored content is being snuck in there, justified by a disclaimer in the fine print. Pelly uncovered through internal documents that Spotify foresees "30–50% of all recommendations on-platform will be influenced by Discovery Mode" in the future.

The unwelcome return of pay-for-play isn't the only problem with the streamers. In the *New Yorker* review of Pelly's book, Hua Hsu suggests that Spotify features "a sizable chunk of the history of recorded music."

This is an oft-repeated idea, particularly by the app's boosters, who might declare, "Why would I pay ten dollars for each album when I could pay the same price for everything ever made?" But imagine *actually* knowing with certainty that you personally had access to nearly everything that has ever come out, the boxes stacked from floor to ceiling filled with crystallized history?

In 2008, Pelly's sister and fellow journalist Jenn Pelly visited Paul Mawhinney's Record-Rama Archive in Pittsburgh, what was considered the world's largest collection of recorded music before it closed that year, in a piece for *Rolling Stone*. "People come in here once in a while, and they ask for a song, and my eyes light up and I feel like I'm part of the human race," said Mawhinney from the dank, windowless confines of Record-Rama in Sean Dunne's 2008 short film *The Archive*. (That year was a transitional time for a music industry that was reeling from piracy. It was also the year that Spotify launched.)

A Library of Congress study determined that 87 percent of Mawhinney's collection, which housed over three million pieces of vinyl and a computer database with over six million song titles, wasn't available on the internet at the time that the film was made. Strictly talking about music that came out between 1948 and 1966, only 17 percent of what Mawhinney collected was ever even available on CD! Some of the stuff at Record-Rama was literally priceless.

The Archive is a lovingly nostalgic look back at what, at the time, felt like a dead medium. It concludes with the familiar sound of surface noise from a needle scratching across the runout groove after a record has ended. Dunne's film commemorated Mawhinney's struggle to find a buyer who could take over the collection. He could no longer maintain it himself, due to complications from diabetes and being legally blind. It's hard to quantify what was at stake with the potential loss of Mawhinney's massive collection, what songs and voices were at risk of being truly forgotten forever without intervention. Brazilian entrepreneur Zero Freitas swooped in to purchase the Record-Rama collection in 2013, bringing his personal collection to over eight million records.

It's impossible to ascertain how many songs have been recorded and released over the course of human history. In a 2014 profile of Freitas in the *New York Times*, a record buyer who worked for him named Allan Bastos estimated that "up to 80 percent of recorded music from the mid-20th century has never been transferred" to digital formats, particularly records from nations such as Cuba, Nigeria, and Brazil.

At press time, Spotify and Apple Music each claim to host over 100 million songs. But neither of the platforms has *Song*, the 1990 sophisti-pop record by Liverpool band It's Immaterial, one of many quality albums that have eluded streaming for various reasons. De La Soul's first six albums weren't digitally available until 2023, due to sample clearance and licensing issues, depriving an entire generation of easy access to several landmark hip-hop albums.

Formerly known as Mos Def, Yasiin Bey released his Grammy-nominated masterpiece *The Ecstatic* in 2009. A vibrant, politically incendiary salvo that has lost none of its potency in the intervening years, it's currently not available on streaming platforms. Your only options for listening to *The Ecstatic* today are a user-uploaded YouTube playlist, illegally downloading it, or finding a physical copy. Having owned the album on vinyl since it was released, I was shocked to learn that copies of that same original pressing were recently going for over eight hundred Canadian dollars apiece on Discogs. The album's absence from streaming has unexpectedly burnished its reputation in the real world, giving *The Ecstatic* a somewhat legendary aura.

In a 2019 interview with *Vibe*, Bey alluded to the situation: "The ownership of that album has come out of the hands of the corporation that owned it, previously. That's why it's not there anymore." On an episode of *The Cutting Room Floor* podcast from 2024, Bey explicitly stated that *The Ecstatic* will never return to Spotify "because what they do over there . . . is an extension of colonialism."

During a visit to the *Drink Champs* podcast in 2022, Bey explained his aversion to putting his releases on streaming by saying, "We're not here to just bow to make things convenient for people per se . . . We're not gonna let the machine set the pace for us." Bey's resistance is admirable. His Madlib-produced collaborative album with Talib Kweli, Black Star's *No Fear of Time*, was released that same year through a podcast platform called Luminary before eventually making its way to Bandcamp.

For his still-unreleased collaborative album with the Alchemist called *Forensics*, Bey sold hats and lanyards on Bandcamp featuring "BUMP™ tag" technology that would provide "discounted access to the full *Forensics* project for digital replay upon its official release" when tapped by your smartphone. Kanye West, now known as Ye, initially released *Donda 2* exclusively on a physical audio device called a Stem Player that he sold on his website in an effort to "free music from this oppressive system" and "take control and build our own." Cindy Lee made a splash with the unconventional strategy of initially releasing their critically acclaimed album *Diamond Jubilee* exclusively on an old-school GeoCities website, eventually pressing it to vinyl. They've since removed their entire discography from Spotify.

When Massive Attack, Godspeed You! Black Emperor, King Gizzard & the Lizard Wizard, Deerhoof, and Xiu Xiu left Spotify in protest of then-CEO Daniel Ek's €600 million investment in military AI technology company Helsing in 2025, some folks were befuddled as to how to listen to these bands off the platform. As more groups inevitably join the exodus from Spotify, the idea of any platform having every song ever made becomes less and less likely.

Unfortunately, not many listeners will make the extra effort to find a record that isn't accessible to them through the channels that they're used to. This is understandable with where we are as a society when it comes to engaging with music technology. According to a 2018 report by Bill Rosenblatt for *Forbes*, digital downloads "lasted for only four years as the leading source of revenue in the recorded music industry," compared to a fifty-eight-year run for vinyl and a twenty-one-year run for CDs. Streaming swooped in and quickly "dispensed with the veneer of ownership entirely . . . for as long as you kept your subscription active."

The Guardian's Alexis Petridis suggests that "streaming encourages a kind of decontextualised discovery . . . where historical context, image, subcultural capital—all the other stuff that was once part of the package—no longer really matters." At the same time, Spotify has trained us to be less curious in how we engage with music by intentionally deprioritizing the search bar in its UX design updates over the years, likely hoping that we will default to its algorithmic playlists.

With the technology claiming to aid music discovery currently falling short, I felt compelled to write a manifesto for digging to remind us all of what we're capable of doing when we sharpen our own instincts. Ever since I was a teenaged record store clerk, I've found great joy in helping people find the music that they always hoped for but never knew how to find. I suggest that you employ some of the habits and attitudes of the digger in your everyday music discovery practice.

The methods that I will outline for you here aren't necessarily an easier way to find music. Unearthing and highlighting obscure tracks is a hard-won way of fighting for the underappreciated, which feels more politically salient than ever in a musical climate where the generic and the palatable are being platformed. My hunt for music feels like a crusade at times, but it's a cause that I deeply believe in.

What I do hope to encourage is less of a reliance on streaming by inspiring you to engage more frequently with physical media and lossless files, both of which keep you in full control of your music library. A rights owner can't remove an album from your hard drive when the license changes hands. A tech company can't stick a thirty-second ad in your face when you turn on your turntable. No one is going to charge you a monthly subscription to use your own vinyl collection (though tech companies absolutely would do this if they could find a way).

The process will likely involve hearing a lot of songs that don't resonate with you at all. Expect some frustration. But this experience will hopefully reconfigure your brain in a way that helps you to more deeply appreciate what you hear on a daily basis going forward, every cab ride or idle moment in a café enlivened by your newfound ways of listening. To truly improve your music listening practice, you need to rethink your entire relationship to the art form.

When I'm in digging mode, I'm relentless. I'll go to a used record shop and spend an hour or more to "clear" the entire place, making sure no corner has been left unturned. It makes me feel like I'm a bottom feeder scouring a seabed. In a good way. I find the process incredibly meditative. It's something I do in every city when I'm on tour. And sometimes the smallest towns have the biggest tracks. I recently found a copy of "Lady Bug" by Bumblebee Unlimited at Zap Records in Kingston, Ontario. The vocals are all pitched up so they sound like insects who are courting each other in a cross-species romance. How on earth did this 1978 novelty disco grail end up in the Limestone City?

Just as reading more books improves your vocabulary and can make your writing more evocative, listening to a broader variety of music can give you access to more specific moods. Early on in my DJ career, I might have played a Caribbean disco record simply because it sounded "tropical." But after expanding my musical language by studying the genre on a deeper level for an extended period of time, I can now find something to play that sounds tropical and languid with a tinge of ennui if the situation calls for it.

I've trained myself to be well equipped for any given moment, giving me more flexibility as a DJ and allowing me to consider more complex textural and emotional combinations when mixing songs together, like an accomplished chef using their advanced technique to cook a weeknight meal for their family.

Whenever I bring home new records that I find on the road, my wife, Sara, and I will ask our toddler son, Yari, if he wants to hear his Record of the Day. He cheers and runs toward the turntable to be my assistant as I twist the needle back onto the tonearm. He'll press the power button on our Pioneer SX-680 stereo receiver (over and over again, of course), and the sound bursts through the speakers into the living room as we all dance together. (Gathering around the Sonos for a Spotify jam session just wouldn't hit the same.) He won't get down to just anything though. Finding funky tunes that will pass the Yari Test has become a rite of passage for any 12-inch hoping to make it into my collection.

The advice I give here is primarily coming from my perspective as a DJ. It can be helpful for breaking anyone out of an algorithmic rut, for reminding us how to take control of our listening after being lulled into technological acquiescence. I'd even argue that my methods for music discovery could be transferrable to hunting for anything, whether it's vintage clothing or any other treasured object. Some of this will be familiar to the music nerds out there. DJs in particular may recognize some of what is written here through their own experience, but hopefully I can conceptualize and articulate these techniques in a way that will be enlightening to even the most jaded dollar-bin diver.

For me, music discovery is a multi-pronged system. Look for new releases in your chosen genres on online merchants like Beatport,

Juno Download, Bleep, and Boomkat. Follow your favourite artists and labels on Bandcamp, social media, and streaming apps so you get alerted to their new releases. For Bandcamp specifically, make sure to go through the collections of other users who bought the same tracks as you. Occasionally, you can stumble on the pages of people who you know in real life as well as professional DJs like Four Tet and see what they're buying.

Check out compilations and reissues in genres that you're interested in. Watch DJs mix on online music platforms like Boiler Room, and learn more about what they played afterwards. I listened to this live mix by Midland from Honcho Campout where he unexpectedly dropped this really abstract remix of Björk's "The Anchor Song" by the Black Dog. It wasn't exactly in my wheelhouse, but it sparked the idea for me to go through every single remix she has ever commissioned. That's how I came across the bugged-out trip-hop of the Motorbass "Transfunk" remix of "Isobel."

Listen to internet radio stations like NTS, n10.as and the Lot Radio. Join promo lists and record pools, services that you can sign up for to get DJ-ready music sent directly to your inbox. Connect with the community on Rate Your Music, and trawl through its exhaustive database. You can find some cool stuff by checking out its charts, such as user-generated ranked lists for obscure subgenres like "Complextro" and "Bongo Flava." If you're looking for a high-quality version of a song and can't find it anywhere, try looking on Qobuz, a digital music store that claims to have "the richest catalogue of hi-res music for streaming and download." Watch documentaries and films about your favourite genres and artists. Stay plugged into music press outlets.

When searching for records, look for the appropriate genres for your location. If I'm in Paris, I keep my eyes peeled for French touch. In New York, disco and garage house should be plentiful. When I slide through

Detroit, I'm likely to come across some techno classics. Use your regional knowledge to your advantage so you can pay less for something when you're in a city that likely had a high historical circulation of a particular record, instead of breaking the bank shelling out for the only copy in town at your local shop.

Try to quickly determine what each record store owner values most. Sometimes you find a store that clearly specializes in rock music. So if you're looking for electro, you already know it's time to keep it moving. A lot of record stores don't care about singles at all. They pay the bills with Sabrina Carpenter variants and are probably happy to off-load their ancient 12-inches to you. Have you ever been to a shop where they cram jazz, blues, hip-hop, reggae, R&B, and disco into the same section? Is all the Black music in the basement? Their prejudice can be your gain! I've come across some amazing records just because a store owner didn't respect a genre enough to properly assess their stock.

Make use of Shazam (an app that can identify songs in just a few seconds) when you're in public and you hear a cool track at a store, coffee shop, or booming out of a passing car. And don't overly fixate on rarity. Spotting undervalued records is a crucial skill of the digger. In Toronto, the crates are lousy with reggae, soca, rap, and R&B singles that are summarily ignored by the techno-craving denizens of the city. I've met U.K. DJs who fly across the ocean to clean up the rare, regionally specific dancehall tracks that are collecting dust in Canadian bins. Listen with your ears, not with your eyes; don't get blinded by the price tag, whether low or high. And don't just grab something you're never going to play because it's worth money. Be a collector, not a speculator.

What exactly am I looking for? The answer changes as I do, but there are a few touchstones that have remained consistent for me. I'm attracted to covers and alternate versions of well-known songs. Playing the right cover song in the club can function as a knowing wink to the audience, a way of saying, "We speak the same cultural language." Covers have the rare combination of feeling familiar while being somewhat destabilizing at the same time, providing an opportunity to surprise and delight the listener.

The other night during my Universal Heartbeat DJ residency in Hamilton at Mills Hardware, I played Ron's "Hai capito o no?" and then mixed in Nashville Rhythm Section's "I Can't Go for That." Both songs are covers of the Hall and Oates classic, sung in Italian and English respectively. The dancers were smiling and laughing together, sharing knowing glances with each other. Decisions like this can be a way to communicate our shared humanity without speaking aloud. It might require a different set of cultural signifiers depending on who you are, who you're playing for, and where you are located, but the meaning behind the act will remain consistent.

Part of the search is knowing what you like and hope to find before you even set out. I know that I have a predilection for disco-adjacent instrumentals with tribal drums. I gravitate toward evocative '80s synth-pop that might call for tears on the dance floor, but I'm also partial to raw electronic sounds, whether it's abrasive industrial sonics paired with pop song structure or the pure machine music of classic Chicago house. I'm an anglophile with a passion for all manner of British music from grime and jungle to '60s pop and '70s lovers rock. Naive, sentimental vocals stir something in me. Be curious about what electrifies you, and take note of the feeling whenever it happens.

We're lucky to have a tool like YouTube that makes exploring what piques your interests easier than ever before. The combo of Discogs and YouTube is pretty much unbeatable for music discovery. Discogs is somewhat like a Wikipedia for music, a user-generated collection of nearly every record ever committed to tape. It's arguably the most comprehensive music database on the internet, sporting a charmingly anachronistic interface that I find cathartic when compared to the over-optimized Web 3.0 hellscape that we're forced to interact with everywhere else. Discogs doubles as a marketplace where collectors and record stores can buy and sell records. The sales data on Discogs is generally how used record stores determine the value and price of what they sell, making it the Kelley Blue Book for vinyl.

If I'm into a particular artist, I'll use Discogs to check out every song they've ever made or worked on. The Shovel for Discogs Chrome extension is a serious time saver, allowing you to add songs to the web browser's side panel for quicker listening. I also explore the output of the producers and engineers who've worked on the tracks that I've loved. Oft-forgotten despite holding a studio role of crucial importance, the mixing engineer in particular can be the hidden link connecting a galaxy of bangers.

Take Alex Sadkin, for instance. Already a connoisseur of artists who've recorded at Compass Point Studios, I took the extra step of hearing everything else that Sadkin has made, and it netted me some cool tracks. Along the way, I learned that Sadkin died in a motorbike accident, leaving the Compass Point community shaken. "Well Well Well" by Grace Jones, Duran Duran's "Do You Believe in Shame?" and Joe Cocker's album *Unchain My Heart* are all dedicated to him. Digging deeper can help us learn that the labour of music-making holds significant meaning beyond its utility and saleability.

Going down a wormhole can lead to great results. When you're searching, follow your intuition. If you find a banging Swedish '80s coldwave track on a compilation, check out other compilations the group has been on and listen to other bands from the same label. Make sure to read the comments on Discogs too. Only the biggest music nerds on earth take the time to post there. And when they do, they often share insights or history about the record you're looking up, occasionally mentioning other relevant tracks or highlighting B-sides that never made it to the streaming platforms. Where there's smoke, there's fire.

If I notice that a few bangers have come from the same label, I'll go to its page on Discogs Marketplace, change the filter to sort by highest price, and then comb through the label's most coveted records. It also lets you search through entire subgenres, combine them for added specificity, and apply various search filters to get granular with your interests. A finely tuned filter will save you time and money in the long run. Looking for the hottest Nigerian disco records released in 1982? No problem.

This can all be a tremendous amount of work, incredibly time-consuming, and sometimes exasperating. There's a lot of guesswork and trial and error involved, hours spent separating the wheat from the chaff, which itself is a skill developed over time. I've spent entire days looking for music only to come away with two or three songs. And occasionally you'll think you've found something, come back to listen again later that afternoon, and you'll have completely changed your mind, repulsed by what the version of you from 11:30 a.m. thought was a banger.

I've learned to move past that initial surge of excitement at unearthing something to coldly assess the true value of a record: Will I still like it in five years? Five days? Five minutes? Some of what I was into a decade ago might not appeal to me today. Pre-pandemic, I was really into acid house. In 2020, I was all about digital dancehall. As my interests shift, so do my targets. Nowadays, I ask myself if a song fits into the sonic profile that I've cultivated for myself up to this point. If red isn't a part of your colour story in your capsule wardrobe, you shouldn't buy big goofy red clown shoes. Records work the same way.

Then again, sometimes I think that I'm not a fan of a whole genre of music when I just haven't yet found the particular variety that resonates with me. For example, I used to think I wasn't a drum and bass guy. But

I kept looking and listening and eventually realized that I specifically gravitate toward liquid and jungle. At this point, I'm seriously considering getting the Moving Shadow logo tattooed on my arm.

It's incredibly rewarding when I strike gold. A track just hits differently when discovering it is the result of effort. And when it comes to hunting for music, the well never goes dry. There's always something new to discover, and the landscape changes as I do. I can feel my taste becoming more expansive and textured after each digging session, the contours around my music knowledge deepening, my discernment sharpening. The amorphous teenager who desperately wanted to work at HMV in West Edmonton Mall so he could get discounts on import-only underground rap CDs would be astonished by what I've discovered as an adult.

One thing that has helped me most is a method that I call "following the breadcrumbs." Here's an example: I'm currently preparing for some summer festival DJ sets. Warm weather puts me in the mood for U.K. garage and disco house, so I've been carving out some time every day to add depth to my crate. I've always enjoyed the funky bounce of German house producer Ian Pooley's 2013 track "Kids Play." I had a couple older songs by him but recently decided to go through all of his releases. During that process, I came across "All Nite," a 1997 single that was exactly what I was looking for.

I've been going through my Rekordbox digital collection on my flash drive and doing spring cleaning as well, erasing tracks that I have no chance of playing again. While doing that, I was reminded of the majesty of DJ Tonka's "Radical Noise," and I realized that I didn't really know any of his other stuff. Over the course of a day spent spelunking through dozens of his songs on YouTube, I found a couple that resonated with me: the scrappy, hypnotic "Feel" and the Daft Punk–ish funk of "She Knows You."

"She Knows You" samples the drum break from Convertion's funky "Let's Do It," an all-time favourite of mine. On Tonka's Discogs page, I noticed one of his remixes was featured on Ian Pooley's 1997 *Live* @ The *Traxx* DJ mix. They had also collaborated with each other on several tracks. I listened to the mix, which led me to discover Pooley's amazing remix of DJ Sneak's "Keep On Groovin'." After these digging sessions, I came away with an assortment of new tracks, further bolstering my collection of a specific genre of music as well as gaining more knowledge of '90s European house.

The difference between passively listening to whatever an algorithm hurls your way and actively searching for music is what you'll find on the way to your destination. I came for some disco house and left with a passing understanding of the German label Force Inc. Music Works. I also discovered some relatively unknown filter house producers by listening to some ancient DJ mixes. I heard some terribly dated records along the way, but those discarded tracks I didn't like helped to establish my taste just as much as finding a song that I love would have done.

If you've settled into the convenience of the streaming era, I'm asking you to totally reconfigure your relationship to the artists you listen to on a deeper level. This is about training yourself to care about the people behind the music as well as the effort that went into making it. Learn about their careers and the connections that they have between each other, immerse yourself in the histories that inform their music and your enjoyment and appreciation of their work will undoubtedly be enriched.

Listen to the universe. When someone mentions a song, save it to a personal playlist. If you hear an amazing oldie at the grocery store, Shazam it. A nerdy guy made an offhand reference to an obscure album he was listening to earlier that day during small talk at a dinner party? Write it down. Recently I was watching a YouTube tutorial and they played a song for a split second. I paused the video, went and found the track, and it was a mind-blowing '90s industrial banger. And then I went and listened to the album it came from, just in case.

Becoming more mindful of capturing the music that usually breezes by us is a way of showing it proper respect. If you live somewhere urban, it can be easy to ignore the cacophonous noise bursting out of passing cars, the tracks blasting out of shops as you pass by. But leaning into the ambient din that soundtracks city life can be similar to taking a moment to appreciate the intricate tile pattern on the walls of your local subway station. Actively choosing to observe the craftsmanship that makes up the scaffolding of modern existence might subtly shift how you engage with everything, not just music.

▶

Back when I was a kid, one of my high school classmates asked me if I was gay when she noticed me listening to *Discovery* by Daft Punk on my navy-blue Panasonic Shockwave during drama class. Such was the stigma around dance music in the early 2000s in Canada, when the average young person's knowledge of the club was limited to what they saw on MuchMusic's *Electric Circus*. The prismatic smorgasbord of genre-defying audio acrobatics that make up *Discovery* was my formative introduction to club music. I was initially snared when I stayed up late to watch Daft Punk's filmic videos for earlier songs like "Da Funk" and "Around the World" on Much's *The Wedge*. There will always be a bit of Thomas and Guy-Man in the DNA of anything I choose to play in the club.

Every music lover or DJ has root artists who act as musical lodestars that they forever refer to. Think of Moodymann's appreciation for Prince, for example. When the *Los Angeles Times* asked the Weeknd about Michael Jackson in 2016, Tesfaye's admiration was clear: "He's everything to me, so you're going to hear it in my music." Bob Dylan's fondness for Woody Guthrie is so well-known that it's become a part of his own legend.

On top of their root artists, DJs often have their own internal logic based on their past experience that dictates what they play. The disc jockey also holds a unique position in nightlife. They are typically the only person in the club who actually has advance knowledge of where the night might go. What makes sense to them might sometimes seem out of left field to the audience, but it works contextually if the dancers know the DJ's backstory or if the jockey's been able to explain it properly through their selections over the span of the night. There's probably a glimmer of Jacques Greene's experience playing hyphy tracks at Zoobizarre as a youth in the back of his mind whenever he plays a set today.

In CCL's Art of DJing feature in online electronic music publication *Resident Advisor*, they talk about having had techno, house, drum and bass, jungle, disco, and dubstep phases in the early part of their career, which likely informs their genre-agnostic style. When you witness a DJ play a song, it isn't just what they decided to spin in that moment. You're also witnessing the weight of experience that brought them to that point.

I started off playing French house and what some people now call "indie sleaze" at house parties and pubs in Edmonton in the late 2000s. My time in Montréal had me playing deconstructed club and italo disco at loft parties, going in on rap and R&B jams at Notre Dame Des Quilles and building a strong library of charcuterie music by playing at restaurants. Living in Toronto, I had to learn how to play dancehall at my night at Parts and Labour. I'd drop Sean Paul's "Get Busy," "No Letting Go" by Wayne Wonder, and Lumidee's "Never Leave You (Uh Oh)" in rapid succession and get the most coveted T-Dot crowd response in return: People started slapping the ceiling.

All of these experiences have helped to make me the music lover that I am today. I carry it all with me every time I play. We rob ourselves of a deeper level of harmony with music when we off-load the taste development process to the algorithms. Streaming apps haven't only devalued music in a monetary sense. They have also gravely damaged cultural appreciation for the art form. What I've written in these pages is a small effort to try to patch up the cracks that have started to show.

We're losing touch with the subtle gradations that dictate exactly how songs are received by our ears: how music can sound different to us when our personal circumstances change, how a sound shifts when we learn the meaning behind it, how our relationship to a song can change over time, and how an artist's actions in the real world can make us perceive their music differently. The richness and subtlety found in the intimacy of listening to music are worth celebrating and protecting. I hope to remind you of the medium's timeless importance, that there are unspoken yet universal feelings connected to our ways of listening just waiting to be committed to the cultural record.

Demoitis

In 1982, Bruce Springsteen caught the most legendary case of demoitis ever.

Maintaining perspective is one of the great challenges in producing music. Demoitis is a common phenomenon among musicians and producers: Someone gets attached to the sound of a particular early version of a song and subsequently becomes resistant to any changes to it. It doesn't matter if a newer mix is technically superior in every way; the artist stays hung up on that old demo.

For the songs that would become 1982's *Nebraska*, Bruce Springsteen recorded a set of acoustic demos on a TEAC 144 Portastudio recorder at his rented ranch house in Colts Neck, New Jersey. Tascam released the Portastudio in 1979. Short for "portable studio," this device allowed musicians to create a four-channel recording and mix it down to cassette tape, all in the comfort of their own homes. For the first time, the average person could affordably record at their house instead of having to save up for expensive studio time. This set off a home-recording revolution, democratizing music and changing the way it would sound for decades to come.

Those *Nebraska* demos were originally made to be fleshed out by the E Street Band at a later date. After failed attempts at recording these songs both with his band and alone in a professional studio, Springsteen made the rare decision to release his demos as the official album. The recording method matched the mood of the record perfectly. The Portastudio cassette demos captured a spare, haunting intimacy that gave Springsteen's hard-luck character studies a chilling edge. This basic consumer-grade equipment somehow facilitated mystically charged performances that couldn't be replicated in a professional recording studio. When Springsteen is asked about who made the choice to put the demos out as an official album in Warren Zanes's book about the making of *Nebraska* called *Deliver Me from Nowhere*, Bruce simply says, "The music itself decided that it was going to come out as it was."

Springsteen was ahead of his time in identifying the beauty in the rawness of demo recordings, which would become de rigueur in the coming years. Homespun bedroom pop and rock sprang forth from the likes of Daniel Johnston, Beck, and Guided by Voices. The revolution reached the world of hip-hop too: Madlib made Quasimoto's *The Unseen* with a Portastudio 488. Wu-Tang Clan bounced the final mixes for *Enter the Wu-Tang (36 Chambers)* from DAT to cassette using a Portastudio 244, cementing the dusty, lo-fi aesthetic that has since become an integral part of the hip-hop tool kit.

Elliott Smith recorded the songs that would become his staggering debut, *Roman Candle*, on a Portastudio 414 in his then-girlfriend JJ Gonson's basement. Unadorned by the usual bells and whistles provided by a professional studio, Smith's heart-rending songs are allowed to shine through clearly. There's an immediacy to these unvarnished recordings; you feel as if you're sitting cross-legged on the ground in front of Elliott himself.

I caught my own case of demoitis just the other day when I was in the studio with Junia-T, who was in the process of replacing samples with live musicians on my album *Forager*. I felt a tinge of sadness that the version I had grown accustomed to, the one I heard countless times driving around the industrial climes of Hamilton, Ontario, would soon be lost forever, with something unfamiliar in its place.

The result of most studio sessions is a state of delusion. Making music can be incredibly empowering. The better you get at creating it, the more you can make the ideas in your head match up with what you end up committing to tape. I'd liken the endorphin rush of bringing forth sound from nothingness to that of taking a chemical substance. This feeling is amplified (pun intended) by those big studio monitors that make everything you play out of them sound like a solid gold hit. But when you go and blast the very same track in your Chevy Equinox a week later, the new song glow has worn off, and the reality is revealed: Your song is actually just *fine*.

Which is okay and something worth celebrating! A song is a song, and to know when one is finished is a valuable skill in itself. Songs aren't released—they escape. But let me let you in on a guilty pleasure of mine: I actually prefer the early versions of songs over the finished tracks I hear on the radio. I love stumbling on embryonic material that helps bring me to fresh conclusions about a beloved track. I enjoy going back and listening to the demos of massive hit songs to chart out how exactly the songwriter made it from point A to point B, to get a clearer glimpse at the journey. Bob Dylan told Cameron Crowe in the liner notes of 1985's *Biograph* compilation that his maligned 1970 double album *Self Portrait* was an intentional attempt at making his "own bootleg record" to combat leaks of his studio sessions. He'd go further with this approach by releasing countless demos and unfinished tracks in his eighteen-part Bootleg Series, including multiple studio takes of the same songs.

But many listeners don't want that. They prefer to pretend that the perfect song was delivered cleanly from the Lord's mouth to the singer's ears, guided by St. Cecilia herself to deftly interpret those heavenly murmurs into heretofore unknown earthly pleasures. For them, there are artists like Beyoncé, notorious for closely guarding her image and output. She has only officially put out one such release, a pristine "original demo" for her song "Sorry."

Many artists guard their early work closely. If you ever have the opportunity to hear an unreleased song that is shared with you by a musician in your life, the click of the spacebar will inevitably be prefaced by a bashful declaration: "It's just a demo!" This is something that I've encountered with every level of musician, from the bedroom experimentalists all the way up to chart-topping superstars. This is particularly ironic when the established artist's more developed skills have made it so that their demos are indistinguishable from the finished product. But alas, the statement will likely be made.

This gesture is partially derived from the perfectionist's urge, but it also comes from a place of anxiety, a common unsteadiness in sharing something that isn't finalized. It's already hard enough to muster the confidence to put yourself out there to the point where you'd be comfortable with letting anyone into your private world. Playing someone an unfinished composition can feel like showing up to a house party without any socks on. There's a chance that no one will notice that you attended a soirée with your toes exposed like Fred Flintstone. But you might fixate on it for the whole night, lingering on an overheard stray comment about someone putting their best foot forward.

The swirling mind of the musician is a uniquely curious thing. It holds the outsized power to create an unimaginable creative bounty that can go beyond what the artist even thought that they were capable of. Simultaneously, the human intellect also comes installed with a doomsday device called insecurity, which can trap and destroy these same ideas within their own grey matter at the first triggering moment, before the music can be freed and heard by the outside world. The music that I make can sometimes sound unfamiliar to my own ears, partly due to the obfuscating power of repetition. I've often heard recording engineers speak of stepping away from a session so that they can come back "with fresh ears."

The changes made to polish these songs before they hit the shelves are usually the correct decisions from a purely commercial perspective. The damaged, raw quality of early versions of songs would likely not make them well-suited for the marketplace. My appreciation of the demo is a purely artistic assessment. The demo is home to the most direct representation of an artist's intentions. I find the demo to have a talismanic quality. They seem to access a pure truth about artistry, opening up a window to the soul that is usually stripped away as the song makes its way through the capitalist meat grinder.

Demos have figured into my own creative process, as I've intentionally made music that has the urgency of early versions of records that I've listened to in the past. The hip-hop radio freestyle is a cousin of the demo, especially when the lyrics are pre-written and intended for placement on a future song, unbeknownst to the world at the time. I'm particularly influenced by raw grime pirate radio recordings such as Dizzee Rascal, Wiley, and Slimzee's Sidewinder Mix on Rinse FM from 2002; that mix is peppered with verses from Dizzee's genre-defining debut *Boy in da Corner* that dropped the next year.

There is a thrill in observing the precise moment when a doodle suddenly gains shape, when vapour takes form seemingly out of nowhere. *The Beatles: Get Back* is a documentary series by Peter Jackson, compiled of found archival footage that asks the question: "Would anyone ever intentionally watch a group jamming for almost eight hours, even if it was the greatest band of all time?" Even a Certified Process Enjoyer like myself struggled to make it through all three parts, but there was one particularly illuminating moment in the first episode.

In the footage from January 1969, it's between ten and eleven in the morning. These Liverpudlians are clearly not morning people. Like those of us watching the series, George is yawning. Ringo is disinterestedly smoking a cigarette. John hasn't shown up yet. Paul begins strumming his bass guitar and hooting aimlessly. The caterwauling turns into wordless singing. George yawns again. And then suddenly Paul somehow springs into the now-unforgettable melody and chorus of "Get Back." It's a eureka moment in real life.

George grows alert and accompanies him on guitar as Ringo starts clapping along and joining in on the chorus. John arrives fashionably late and joins the jam in progress. We're watching history in motion. I've never seen a better representation of the abruptness with which nothing can turn into something in the world of music. *The Beatles: Get Back* treats us to a rare live example of a demo being crafted out of thin air.

▶

Short for "demonstration tape," a demo wasn't, initially, anything that you or I would actively seek out to listen to. It was purely a means to an end, a bare-bones recording of a song designed to serve a specific pre-release purpose. Before a musician had a record deal, they would create a demo using whatever cheap equipment they had in their garage and then send it to a record label. Demos were about trying to capture what a band sounded like when they played live.

Hopefully, an A&R representative would fish the offering out of the towering pile of discs and cassettes, get blown away by the songs, and then sign the band, who would finally be able to make some real music in a professional studio with a producer. De La Soul rapped about being haunted by desperate aspiring emcees hawking such demo tapes on their 1991 single "Ring Ring Ring (Ha Ha Hey)." Madlib and his alter ego Quasimoto threw subpar demos out of their car window on 2005's "Another Demo Tape."

In the early days of home recording, established acts would make demos to test out their new equipment, such as on Paul McCartney's experiment "Check My Machine." Musicians would make demos to get their often-ephemeral ideas down quickly so they could later be shared with their collaborators. Coming across the watery drum machine demo for "Baker Street" on YouTube, I was amazed to hear that the song's unforgettable hook was initially played by Gerry Rafferty on wah-wah guitar before he tapped Raphael Ravenscroft to reproduce it as a now-iconic saxophone part. Michael Jackson famously recorded himself beatboxing, humming melodies, and demonstrating vocal harmonies at home before he would step foot in the studio, as illustrated on the demo for "Beat It."

One of my favourite demos ever is the one made for "I Missed Again" by Phil Collins. Originally titled "I Miss You, Babe" and written about his first wife, Andrea Bertorelli, leaving him, the demo features minimal accompaniment: a simple drum machine loop with a delay effect on it, chiming reverb-drenched blues piano, and a distant synthesizer as Collins sings his heart out about the dissolution of his marriage. The chillingly elegiac tone is perfect on this intimate solo recording. It feels frozen in time, like a framed wedding photograph.

For the studio version, Collins decided to change up the lyrics and atmosphere of the song. In a 1999 episode from the TV program *Classic Albums* about his album *Face Value*, Collins said he wanted to make the song "funnier" and "ironic," retreating from the vulnerable sorrow of the demo. Somewhat unsurprisingly, world-famous Genesis drummer

Phil Collins replaced the brittle drum machine sounds with a smashing full kit. A victim of the '80s predilection for overproduction, "I Missed Again" features a sensual tenor saxophone solo by U.K. jazz luminary Ronnie Scott and an R&B horn section jaggedly puncturing the composition at random intervals in a somewhat cheesy attempt at a Tower of Power funk moment.

Conversely, another Collins song, "In the Air Tonight," actually tracks quite closely to the demo made during the original 1979 sessions, both anchored by the same Roland CR-78 drum machine Disco-2 preset and eerie Prophet-5 synth pads. These exact demo instrumental performances were retained and used on the studio version, while the vocals were rerecorded. The final version also includes a vital new addition: possibly the most famous drum fill in the history of recorded music, without which the song would not feature the striking contrast that helped turn it into a timeless classic.

What if Collins and co-producer Hugh Padgham had decided to swap out the drum machine for live drums on the studio version? What if they'd opted to make the song into an upbeat affair like they had with "I Missed Again?" The life of a producer is littered with these choices, and they can often be the difference between failure and success. It's possible that "In the Air Tonight" might not have been made at all if not for the presence of the Roland drum machine that allowed Collins, as he told *Mix* magazine, to "start writing some of this music that was inside me."

Every demo holds inside it unlimited possibilities, each a memorial to that temporary state of the creative process when decisions remain tantalizingly unmade. As the demo shifted away from its initial role as an industry tool for demonstration, it incrementally became a tent pole of the creative process, providing the perfect landscape for bands to experiment. And nothing made that more possible than the advent of the drum machine.

Much like how the Portastudio made it feasible to cut a proper demo at home instead of needing to go to a professional studio, early programmable drum machines like the Roland CR-78, the Boss Dr. Rhythm DR-55, and the Linn LM-1 allowed musicians to add rhythmic accompaniment to their rough recordings without hiring a live drummer. Their use was initially purely functional, but over time, the aesthetic value of the drum machine became impossible to ignore.

Phil Collins described this development in detail when he explained why he kept the CR-78 on the studio version of "In the Air Tonight" on *Classic Albums*: "The whole thing was set up by the mood of this drum machine for me. When you hear that, you couldn't possibly replace that with real drums. You know, people say, 'Why do you use a drum machine when you're a drummer?'. . . It's the atmosphere, it's relentless, it doesn't move. A drummer would get bored playing anything like this."

Demo recordings had a major part in legitimizing drum machines as a compositional tool for a new generation of adventurous artists. The DR-55 provided the dark beatbox percussion for New Order's "Truth" and the Cure's "One Hundred Years," making it a sonic signifier for the early '80s new wave scene. Depeche Mode's Dave Gahan used it in their early live shows, and it was also present on proto-techno tracks like Cybotron's "Clear." Prince's mastery of the Linn LM-1 was a significant aspect of what made his sound so unique. Soft Cell featured the CR-78 on 1981's "Tainted Love." And as more robust drum machines emerged, so did entire music genres along with them.

Inspired by the hypnotic drive of Giorgio Moroder and Donna Summer's disco masterpiece "I Feel Love," Blondie created "Heart of Glass," a watershed moment in the history of pop music. Unlike most of the drum machine stories I've mentioned so far, "Heart of Glass" didn't start with one. "Once I Had a Love (a.k.a. the Disco Song)" was what the band called the first demo that they made back in 1975, when they were first starting out. It was a song that they'd struggled with for years, telling *The Guardian* that they'd "tried it as a ballad, as reggae, but it never quite worked."

The demo feels much slower than the song we all know, marrying downtown New York funk-punk to a half-time tropical bounce reminiscent of West African palm wine guitar music, recalling the mood of other New York songs from that era such as "Charley's Girl" from Lou Reed's *Coney Island Baby*. A prominent lyric finds Debbie Harry puckishly describing a failed relationship as being a pain in the ass.

A second demo was recorded at the Record Plant in New York on June 3, 1978, featuring a more amped-up tempo, a boilerplate disco beat, a new instrumental section with a 7/4 time signature change, and the now-famous main guitar riff. Blondie only revisited the song after *Parallel Lines* producer Mike Chapman asked them if they had any additional material before they started sessions for that album. On this version, the band's pop ambitions have become clearer with the reference to the pain in the ass happening only once at the end, while the relationship is referred to as something from the past everywhere else.

As they hack away at it on these demos, you can hear Blondie cracking the puzzle, piece by piece. On the final studio version released in 1979, the lyric that they'd been tinkering with was altered once again, this time by Chris Stein. He came up with a gorgeously poetic turn of phrase that perfectly matched the song's new sonic backdrop, bringing to mind a hard, transparent, vulnerable object that could be mistaken for love itself: a heart of glass.

The CR-78 drum machine is here now, the introduction for "Heart of Glass" sporting a combination of the Mambo and Beguine presets, providing an inimitable plastic heartbeat for drummer Clem Burke to play his kit along to. In a precursor to MIDI technology, the CR-78's trigger out function was used in conjunction with a Roland SH-5 to create the song's stuttering synth bass line.

Harry's voice is treated with a cosmic delay that gives her singing an android sheen. What was once a punk band sheepishly toying with a disco sound palette had become a pop group making their star turn by going all in on passionate eurodisco. For listeners back in 1978, hearing it over the airwaves must have been like cresting a wave on a schooner with a new world on the horizon. The drum machine supercharged Blondie's creativity, lending the finishing touch to a timeless single that went number one in eight countries.

▶

From out of a trembling wall of crackling hiss emerges a loop of a man cooing melodically, double-tracked to resemble a chorus of more than one person. Soon, these vocalizations are overshadowed by a gentle voice singing a surprisingly profane provocation in a buoyant falsetto. Unexpectedly aggressive for what is ostensibly an R&B track about lost love, the words are not sung in a confrontational manner; rather, they are done in a half-remembered, self-possessed warbling style that sounds more likely to be belted out alone in the shower than on an artist's debut single.

A sloppy-sounding, unquantized kick drum thuds away, suddenly joined by a loud clap sound. Like two hands ripping the songwriting rulebook in half, what sounds like a distorted Roland Juno-60 synth line punctures the mood, plopping us firmly into the sound world of Jai Paul on "BTSTU (Demo)." The song melds a jarring contrast of hard and soft with the use of a limited sonic palette in the most maximal of ways.

Part of Paul's success with "BTSTU" is how he put together familiar elements in an unlikely manner. Pop songs in 2010 didn't typically feature bounding J Dilla–inspired drums that grooved like a pair of boots being thrown down the stairs. An effect designed to give club tracks their pumping rhythm by muting other sounds when a kick comes in, sidechain compression was considered the domain of house music, not funk, R&B, or whatever this was. Paul randomly cuts out elements of his own track as it progresses as if he's a pirate radio DJ going in on the faders. Hearing these elements simultaneously in a song that was already difficult to classify felt foreign and unnerving.

The song's surprising saxophone coda delivers a human richness that works better than it should when considering the music that preceded it. The chiming guitar mixed with falsetto vocals are reminiscent of Prince and D'Angelo, but perfectionists of their standard would have never allowed a track this shaggy to see the light of day. This was the sound of one man's singular melodic logic, all created using methodology that would be considered incorrect enough to get him failed by any music production school.

As a user on audio engineering message board Gearspace put it, "He sounds like he produces his music high on meth." Like an unfinished demo that has yet to be properly mixed, Paul's vocals are intentionally low in the mix to the point of being unintelligible. It's a rare song that forces us to parse it in real time. This sensation gave me the curious feeling that I was chasing after Paul with my ears, akin to trying to catch a firefly in a jar at night, forcing me to grasp for stray information as I played the song on repeat. I've been listening to it for over a decade now, and the track's words and meaning still remain thrillingly opaque to me.

"BTSTU (Demo)" was discovered on Paul's unassuming Myspace page in 2010. The plain language and humble attitude displayed on his social media page belied the world-beating tenor of his music: "whats goin on my names jai im a artist/producer jst startin out in the game let me kno if u feel it . . . thanks 2every1 whos been backin me I rly appreciate it peace jai." But the more we gleaned about him, the more Paul showed himself to be an inscrutable figure. *Pitchfork*'s Lindsay Zoladz would describe him as being "as secretive and enigmatic as Burial and as press-averse and slow-working as Terrence Malick."

The song set the blogosphere on fire, leading to an official remastered release as "BTSTU (Edit)" via iconic U.K. independent label XL Recordings in 2011 after a bidding war. Taste-making DJ Zane Lowe named it the Hottest Record in the World on BBC, Drake sampled it for "Dreams Money Can Buy," and Beyoncé flipped the song's intro on "End of Time." Paul was tapped to produce and sing on Big Boi from OutKast's "Higher Res" in 2012, crafting a warped, tumbling rhythm and towering dub-like bass for one of hip-hop's bravest adventurers.

The world's biggest stars were captivated by this unpolished, seemingly incongruent music that completely defied categorization but still held addictive pop songwriting at its core. Jai Paul's rampant rule-breaking sounded like freedom to the manicured mainstream. But these attempts by major label hitmakers to harness Paul's wild energy failed to elicit the same thrills as his own output.

In his only ever interview, conducted by Michael Cragg for *Dazed* magazine in 2012, Paul claimed to have made "BTSTU" at home in Rayners Lane in northwest London in less than an hour. World domination was not on his mind; he was just vibing and making tunes. "I didn't think anyone would like it though," he said. "Music to me was just a hobby and, in a way, I didn't care about showing it to anyone." This uncommon composition came from a quirky creator who was happily out of touch: He didn't use an iPod, had never even heard of iTunes, and exclusively listened to the pop music of his childhood, which included Michael Jackson, Queen, the Beatles, and Electric Light Orchestra.

For quite some time, there was only one image of him in circulation: a collage featuring a bedroom selfie in which he's rocking a 1995/1997 Chelsea home football jersey, an Adidas track jacket, and blue makeup under his eyes. When the full photo was posted by Paul in a rare 2021 Instagram post to celebrate ten years of "BTSTU," I noticed that he was flanked by posters of a somewhat unlikely array of worldwide pop inspirations: Alicia Keys, Kylie Minogue, Basement Jaxx, and Amy Winehouse.

Jai Paul's second single, "Jasmine (Demo)," was released in 2012 via SoundCloud. Opening with a repetitive synth bass pulse that recalls the intros of "Eye of the Tiger" and "Edge of Seventeen" if they were played from five hotel rooms over, watery guitar figures dance delicately between Paul's fragile, unplaceable whispers. The reverberant profile of the song implies a haunted love affair, as rumbling samples and echo-drenched claps ripple across the landscape of the beat like chairs being pulled across the kitchen in *Poltergeist*. The song was covered by Ed Sheeran, and *Pitchfork* named it Best New Track.

Despite being released by vaunted indie label XL Recordings, the song arrived appended with "(Demo)" at the end of the title. Perhaps this was a way of heading off potential criticism of work that he still considered incomplete when he delivered it to the label. Or was it a mark of pride, as if to say that his demos were better than most people's finished songs? Either way, this turned out to be a watershed moment in which a musician used the unfinished nature of their releases as a marketing tool.

Unfortunately, his celebration of the work-in-progress would eventually lead to great distress. The next year, a collection of his demos was uploaded to Bandcamp without song titles and sold as if it was Jai Paul's debut album. The usually tight-lipped Paul tweeted, "To confirm: demos on bandcamp were not uploaded by me, this is not my debut album. Please don't buy. Statement to follow later. Thanks, Jai," and XL Recordings subsequently confirmed that it was not an official release.

The music world didn't quite know how to deal with the situation. Some critics thought it was an intentional stunt to drum up media attention. Paul had released demos before; why couldn't he have done it again? Fans couldn't decide whether or not it was ethical to listen to unfinished music against the will of the person who created it. The songs were so compelling that publications like *Pitchfork* and *The Guardian* still included the unofficial release on their year-end lists.

While his demos were being celebrated, Paul basically disappeared. Over the next few years, his sound as presented on the leak was picked over for parts by both bedroom producers and the mainstream alike. During his hiatus, he started the Paul Institute label with his brother A.K., and they released singles by other artists. A rare photo of him and his brother wearing hi-vis vests and hard hats was included in *Property Week* magazine, in a news article about the purchase of their label office in White City in 2017.

Six years after the leak, Paul finally resurfaced with a statement explaining that the tracks were a hodgepodge of recordings in varying degrees of completion "from roughly 2007 to 2013" that likely came from "a burned CD that got misplaced." Paul described the mental anguish of having his life's work sold to the public without his consent, referring to it as "a catastrophe" that led to "a significant loss of trust." No one believed that he hadn't leaked the demos himself. He spent years having to explain his side of the story repeatedly. Paul had a breakdown and went through therapy in order to "acknowledge some of the trauma and grief" that beset him after having his demos leaked.

In 2019, he was ready to take back ownership of the narrative around these songs by putting them out officially on XL Recordings as *Leak 04-13 (Bait Ones)*. To paraphrase some lyrics from "BTSTU," he was back and he wanted what was his. It was finally Paul's turn to reap the rewards of an album that had become the source material for so many records in its wake. The remastered *Bait Ones* retains the same track order as the leak, meaning the album's sequencing was decided by the complete stranger who sold his demos online.

There was a sense of relief to see these incomplete compositions added to the public record as a proper release and still retain their raw ingenuity. Other than "Jasmine," "BTSTU," the interludes, and the blistering Bollywood funk track "Str8 Outta Mumbai," the album's tracks are each tagged with "(Unfinished)." "It will always be a little painful for me to listen to myself, but I don't want to deny people a chance to hear it, especially as it's already knocking about," Paul said in his statement.

The final stop on Jai Paul's redemption tour was the earth-shattering news that he would be playing his first show ever at Coachella in 2023. Was this actually going to happen? How would his fragmented, production-heavy songs translate live? I remember logging on to the livestream from my hotel room in Saskatoon after I had performed at Remai Modern, rapt with anticipation. I was warmed by the obvious love and reverence that the crowd had for this reclusive figure who had made his mark on music history but lacked the name recognition of headlining draws like Bad Bunny and Frank Ocean.

Wearing a blond bob wig and space age shades, Jai Paul performed a variety of songs from *Bait Ones* with full band accompaniment as he wandered around a set decorated with rock formations. Hearing the songs in this context, I realized that this might have been what he intended for the finished version of his album to sound like, had it not been leaked. On this stage, the songs read a bit more conventionally as straight R&B, the group's funky licks occasionally bringing the tracks uncomfortably close to late-night-TV band territory.

Hearing the songs without the ornamentation of his production for the first time was a bit like peeking behind the curtain at a magician's show. And then it hit me: I was suffering from demoitis for Jai Paul's discography. My perception of how his music was *supposed to sound* was preventing me from appreciating the actual songs in live form. I realized that part of the joy of his output was in not knowing exactly what I was hearing. On the Coachella stage, the low volume of his vocals came off more as a lack of confidence than the intentional creative decision it is on the recordings.

Whether something is completed or a demo can only truly be decided by the person who made it. In tagging his songs' official titles with "Demo" and "Unfinished," Paul drew a line between the professional demos he considered worthy of releasing and the unreleased sketches that were taken from him and shared without his approval. That the public couldn't tell the difference didn't hamper his legacy. Jai Paul will forever be seen as the artist who knowingly elevated the demo to a new stature in the public consciousness.

▶

In a streaming era when deluxe versions of albums with bonus tracks are now industry standard, demos have become invaluable tools for extending a release's life cycle in an oversaturated marketplace. This has led to some remarkable discoveries. Anniversary editions of classic albums come loaded with unreleased tracks and never-before-heard demos that are culturally significant, such as the Super Deluxe Edition of Prince's *Diamonds and Pearls* that spans seven discs of mostly previously unheard material. It's a pleasure to be living in a time when early versions of classic songs are now readily shared with us in high fidelity.

Conversely, Taylor Swift's weaponization of her demos by adding them to limited edition digital versions of *The Tortured Poets Department* in what appeared to be an attempt to block Billie Eilish's *Hit Me Hard and Soft* from the top spot on the *Billboard* 200 highlights how the demo's inherent purity can be perverted, especially now that their saleable utility has become so well-known by the music industry. Taylor's so-called First Draft Phone Memos were presumably recorded using only her piano and her iPhone. Constructing a false atmosphere of performative intimacy by speaking to her future imagined audience on the recordings, it's transparently obvious that these voice memos were always intended to later be used as bonus material.

We've moved past the demo as marketing tool into an era when the demo is being used as genuine proof of the labour that lies behind the creative process. Today's artists want to be associated with the production process in a way that they didn't in the past. The listening public knew exactly what Drake intended to signal by naming his 2020 release *Dark Lane Demo Tapes*: It wasn't a proper album but a collection of odds and ends to tide fans over until his next full-length. Same thing with Kendrick Lamar's *untitled unmastered*.

Chillwave producers and lo-fi indie rock bands in the late 2000s deliberately made their music sound more like demos to mimic the raw sound of the vintage tunes they grew up on. Mac DeMarco first garnered mainstream attention after releasing the intentionally scrappy *Rock and Roll Night Club*, which was made with a Portastudio 244 in his first-floor apartment of the building where we both lived in Montréal. A *New Yorker* profile ahead of his 2025 album *Guitar* pointed out how demoitis factored into DeMarco's process, remarking on how he "spends most of his time in the studio chasing after the magic of that first iteration."

While mainstream artists use demos to prove that they actually make their own music, underground acts embrace the sonic signifiers of the demo to emphasize their uniqueness and down-to-earth nature when compared to their major-label counterparts. The democratization of the demo via home recording has reached an inflection point since the days of the Portastudio. With applications like GarageBand, Pro Tools, and Ableton paired with the increased processing power of modern computers, anyone with the resources can make as many home demos as they want without restrictions. There are communities of musicians on Discord who hang out online and share works-in-progress every day.

For the first time ever, it's become remarkably easy to access the exact same plugins and gear that your favourite artists use.

The consumer-as-artist boom has also led to further curiosity around the techniques that the pros use to make their chart-topping music in a now-oversaturated industry; tutorials like "How to Make DANCE POP Music (like Charli xcx's *Brat*)" are posted to YouTube. This interest could be connected to artists taking fans behind the scenes by sharing their unreleased tracks on social media and elsewhere. Charli and producers George Daniel and A.G. Cook even pulled back the curtain themselves by explaining the process of making *Brat* on the *Tape Notes* podcast.

Ye in particular has blurred the line between demo and official release since 2016's *The Life of Pablo*, turning his album rollouts into an interactive experience for his fans. The *Pablo* rollout culminated in an epic listening party on February 11, 2016, at Madison Square Garden that was livestreamed on Tidal and doubled as a fashion show for season three of Ye's Yeezy clothing brand. West was surrounded by famous peers like Pusha T, 2 Chainz, and Kid Cudi in front of a still-unsurpassed spectacle of models and celebrities suspended on pillars while draped in splashes of muted colour.

Ye shared these cutting-edge, never-before-heard songs through humble means: *The Life of Pablo* was played through an aux cord connected to Ye's laptop. You can hear computer sound effects and the telltale static when the cable is plugged in and out. We now know that what was heard that night was an unfinished version of the album, making this possibly the largest scale example of someone sharing their demos with some friends.

The album was released three days later, but Ye didn't stop tinkering, posting the classic tweet "Ima fix wolves" after fans complained about preferring an earlier leaked version. He did, in fact, fix "Wolves" over a month later by re-adding verses from Sia and Vic Mensa and making

Frank Ocean's ending into a separate song called "Frank's Track." He also changed a lyric on "Famous" around that time. On March 30, forty-five days after *Pablo* was originally released, there was a major update to ten tracks on the album, ranging from mixing changes to new versions of verses and even different arrangements for some songs. The updates continued sporadically, ending with a completely new song called "Saint Pablo" being added to the end of the album on June 14.

Treating the album format as a living document that can be given system updates like an Apple operating system was a novel, even thrilling, approach at the time. This was arguably the first time an artist could put out an album, listen to the audience's feedback, and then go back to make changes. The art was no longer static. Unfortunately, the freedom to alter his tracks became a slippery slope for Ye as the years went on. His music has become more fractured and incomplete-sounding with each successive release, a surprising turn for the noted perfectionist behind incredibly well-thought-out classics like *My Beautiful Dark Twisted Fantasy*.

Listening back to *Vultures 1* as I write this, I've noticed that a song I once liked has since been dramatically altered. I feel as if I can't trust my own ears because the artist can't trust his own decisions. The release of *Vultures 2* was marred by poor mixing, and songs like "530" initially featured mumbled scratch verses where Ye rapped the kind of nonsense you typically hear on rap demos. Countless changes have since been made to that album with more songs being added. A few of Ye's verses on *Vultures 2* are credibly rumoured to be other people rapping with a Ye AI filter over their voice. This is the sound of an artist who has lost his discernment, a businessman treating his art purely as a product to be patched and updated if poorly received by consumers.

With access to leaked and unreleased tracks becoming more commonplace, we're in a time when songs are scrutinized every step of the way before they're officially released. Travis Scott had a "Wolves" moment when his single "4x4" came out with vocal mixes that were criticized by fans. He tweeted, "I fixed the mix bruh lol," and the song was updated on all platforms. But along with the mixing changes, an instrumental outro featuring a Tay Keith producer drop was removed. I had already grown attached to this ending and mourned its loss, the blank space paved over like a pothole on the highway.

Now that the idea of a song sounding intentionally unfinished has been normalized and absorbed into the tool box of every level of musician, the demoitis that brought us Bruce Springsteen's *Nebraska* has been replaced with a sort of demophilia: a state of mind where a song can be endlessly tinkered with and updated with no regard for the audience's attachment to a previous version. We could be entering an era where two people might fall in love with completely different iterations of the same track, permanence be damned.

Not Like Us

"No way," I exclaimed to my DJ, Josephine.

It was the morning of April 30, 2024, and we had just landed in drizzly Montréal ahead of a few East Coast performances. After tossing our Rimowas into the trunk of our Uber, I sat in the back seat and loaded up X as we pulled out of the airport.

After more than two weeks of silence, Kendrick Lamar had responded to Drake's disses. I fumbled for my AirPods and crammed them into my ears. As the song played, I paused occasionally to give a play-by-play to Josephine as if we were watching a horror movie and she was covering her eyes.

"Kendrick just called Drake a master manipulator and a habitual liar."

"He just made a reference to YNW Melly."

"Oh my God, he's doing the Toronto accent now!"

The song in question was "Euphoria," and it rocked the world, breaking the single day streaming record for a 2024 hip-hop song and eventually hitting number three on the *Billboard* Hot 100 chart. To the casual observer, this public airing of grievances between megastars seemed as if two random artists from their Spotify playlist had inexplicably gotten into a tiff. But make no mistake, this cold war of words had been simmering in the background for over a decade.

The conflict reached a fever pitch in late 2023 when J. Cole and Drake released "First Person Shooter," in which J. Cole attempted to lay out the hierarchy of hip-hop and claim himself and Drake as two of the big three in the genre. Lamar returned fire in March 2024 on Future and Metro Boomin's blistering "Like That," an extract from their album dedicated to Drake's allegedly mendacious nature entitled *WE DON'T TRUST YOU*. On "Like That," Kendrick flatly rejected J. Cole's assessment, asserting his own primacy as the best rapper alive.

Kendrick Lamar and Drake represent two contrasting paths to stardom befitting their recent references to being the Prince and Michael Jackson of their generation, respectively. One got to the top by pushing the art form of rap in new and unexpected directions, while the other did it by mastering the pop formula and breaking chart records in the process. This is a battle not only between two individuals but also two divergent musical ideologies.

▶

I distinctly remember the shift when being a Canadian rapper went from being an oddity to a commodity. Back when I was studying at Hampton University in Virginia, I remember telling the kids in my dorm that I rhymed, and they were stunned by the idea of a rapping Canadian. They laughed until they heard me perform and begrudgingly showed me some respect. When I first started professionally releasing music as Cadence Weapon in the mid-2000s, Canada's hip-hop landscape was much different and less prominent in the public consciousness than it is today. Outside Toronto, you really had to go out of your way to know what was happening with rap in the country. I ran into much resistance in those years, relegated to performing on festival bills alongside an army of white indie rock bands and a shocking lack of racial and gender diversity.

Everything changed after Drake blew up. Suddenly, every interviewer was clamouring to talk about the country's hip-hop scene, wanting to know my opinion of the new superstar. His shadow loomed larger and larger until it seemingly blocked the world's view of the rest of us, like the moon eclipsing the sun. The pioneers who came before, like Maestro Fresh Wes, Michie Mee, and Kardinal Offishall, became footnotes in his story. Every rapper in Canada was judged by how they compared to Drake and his megastardom, even if they weren't shooting for the same goal.

Aubrey Drake Graham had to endure wave after wave of humiliation on his way to the top. Growing up mixed and middle class in Toronto's affluent Forest Hill neighbourhood, he found success as a child actor on *Degrassi: The Next Generation*. As a result, he wasn't taken seriously when attempting to make the unlikely shift to legitimate hip-hop artist. His own country largely ignored him and his mixtapes until he was signed by Lil Wayne in 2009, which brought him instant credibility and sparked his meteoric rise.

Like most young artists, he was derivative of others at first. His oscillation between punchline raps and melodic singing made him sound like a cross between Little Brother's Phonte and Ye circa *808s & Heartbreak*. But as the years went by, he carved out his own sonic formula, which he mastered on 2011's *Take Care*: a claustrophobic study in longing that catered to an audience who mistook a man rapping about his feelings to be a sign of emotional intelligence. This stood out in the macho world of rap.

With his rise came growing pains. He was publicly embarrassed on the night he hosted the Junos in 2011 when he didn't win in any of his six nominated categories. Drake stopped submitting his albums for Juno consideration after 2016's *Views* didn't win a single award out of five nominations. Despite having sold over 223 million records worldwide and won five Grammys over the span of his career, critical appreciation has largely eluded him. But with each successive hit album, his outsized influence on Canada and the country's rap scene grew.

Through sheer determination, Drake arguably made being Canadian cool. He brought the Toronto accent to the mainstream in a sketch on *Saturday Night Live*. He sat on the edge of the CN Tower for the cover of *Views*. A *VICE News* report determined that Drake was solely responsible for "about 5 percent of the city's $8.8 billion total annual tourism income" (roughly $440 million) in 2018, derived from his role as global ambassador for the Toronto Raptors, his music, and his local references.

His annual OVO Fest became a pilgrimage event for African Americans. Building on the foundation developed over decades by Toronto's Afro-Caribbean diaspora, Drake celebrated the true spirit of a city that famously existed in the cultural memory as a generic stand-in for New York and Chicago in films. Along with the Weeknd and PARTYNEXTDOOR, Drake is chiefly responsible for what has been referred to as the Toronto sound: dark, intimate, R&B-inflected rap seemingly designed for driving down the Gardiner at night.

Drake brought the ephemera of Toronto to the masses on an unprecedented scale, turning him into a local hero in the process. All across the city, he had us proudly screaming about running through the Six with our woes. Starting with his guest verse on "Versace" by Migos in 2013, Drake went on a run of features that led to a popularity boost for the artists he collaborated with that was dubbed "the Drake effect." His success, cultural impact, and elevated status insulated him to the point that he felt comfortable confronting other rappers, marking a pivotal shift in Drake's identity.

With 2015's *If You're Reading This It's Too Late* and his disses to Meek Mill from the same year, Drake presented a more aggressive, angrier approach to rapping that seemed, to outsiders, to come out of nowhere. But it made sense to local hip-hop fans who were aware of his support for battle rap leagues like King of the Dot, which he co-hosted in 2011 and 2013. He flirted with actually competing in the battle scene over the years, even going as far as saying "I study rap battles for a living," as a guest on LeBron James's HBO show *The Shop* in 2018.

Ghostwriting accusations by Meek on Twitter poked some holes in Drake's credibility, but "Back to Back" cemented Drake as a battle rapper to be reckoned with. The song was a rare diss track that garnered significant commercial success, going double platinum and peaking at number twenty-two on the *Billboard* Hot 100. It has stood the test of time, landing at the eighth spot on *Complex*'s 2024 list of the fifty best hip-hop diss songs of all time. Following "Back to Back," Drake continued to painstakingly construct a reality where his pop success meant he should be considered the greatest rapper in the game. He progressively shifted away from his lovelorn crooning Lothario persona, transforming into something of a globe-trotting mob boss figure.

His 2018 battle with Pusha T, spurred by an earlier disagreement between Clipse, the Neptunes, and Lil Wayne, resulted in the revelation that Drake was hiding a previously undisclosed child, which damaged his image but had little impact on his commercial success. He followed the conflict with massive hits like "In My Feelings" and "Sicko Mode." But by the time of 2023's *For All the Dogs*, the vulnerability that had once made him beloved by women had largely faded into casual misogyny, attracting a new fanbase of angry young men.

▶

Kendrick Lamar Duckworth was the chosen one from the very beginning. A child prodigy with a rough Compton upbringing who was artistically fostered by Dr. Dre, Kendrick's place in hip-hop culture has always been secure. In 2011, he was symbolically passed the torch by West Coast hip-hop forefathers Snoop Dogg, Kurupt, Daz, Warren G, and the Game onstage at the House of Blues as he cried tears of joy. That same year, Kendrick was brought on tour by an already-ascendant Drake and featured on "Buried Alive Interlude" from 2011's *Take Care*. His 2012 major label debut *good kid, m.A.A.d city* was heralded as an instant classic, with Drake stopping by to drop a verse on "Poetic Justice."

Kendrick's music received worldwide universal acclaim for its seamless blend of vivid storytelling, conceptual depth, and ferocious rapping. It spoke to West Coast street culture effortlessly, tapping into the verbiage and customs of his community. He had grown up on welfare and seen someone murdered in a drive-by shooting outside his Section 8 apartment when he was five years old. When he was eight, his father brought him to the Compton Swap Meet so he could watch Tupac and Dr. Dre film the video for "California Love." This is the duality that informs his music.

But the turning point in his career was his incendiary 2013 verse on Big Sean's "Control," where he threw down the gauntlet and called out the biggest rappers in the game by name. This was pure hip-hop gamesmanship where to be the best, you have to beat the best. Most of the rappers mentioned took it as a compliment. But Drake was clearly offended when he responded in a *Billboard* cover story: "I know good and well that Kendrick's not murdering me, at all, in any platform. So when that day presents itself, I guess we can revisit the topic."

Kendrick followed that salvo up with a dazzling BET cypher verse in which he seemingly jabbed Drake directly. His 2015 effort *To Pimp a Butterfly* was even more virtuosic: a dizzying, introspective blend of funk and jazz with a recurring motif that eventually leads to him having a full conversation with the ghost of Tupac himself. It featured one of his signature songs, "Alright," which became a protest anthem for the Black Lives Matter movement.

2017's *DAMN.* landed like a thunderbolt and earned Kendrick the 2018 Pulitzer Prize for Music and his first *Billboard* number one solo single, "Humble." A swirling religious allegory about damnation, *DAMN.* swings between being meditative and almost unbearably intense. The record was so painstakingly crafted that it was designed to be played forward and backwards without losing conceptual integrity.

Kendrick has since become the flag bearer for conscious rap, a master of a dying art form. He has cemented his status as one of the greatest rappers of his generation. Despite being a commercial and critical darling, Kendrick has always been a knotty, curious artist who has carefully walked the balance between art and commerce, usually landing firmly on the former side of the divide. 2022's *Mr. Morale & the Big Steppers* was a challenging listen that explores Kendrick's infidelity as well as themes of abuse. While it didn't initially resonate with a mainstream audience, it helped to cement his status as hip-hop's moral compass.

▶

The history of hip-hop is filled with petty disagreements that ended up being committed to wax. Roxanne Shanté invented the hip-hop answer song in 1984 with "Roxanne's Revenge," a response to UTFO's misogynistic "Roxanne, Roxanne" track about a fictional woman. Shanté's song led to a craze called the Roxanne Wars, involving anywhere between thirty and over one hundred Roxanne-related diss tracks by at least thirty-five different artists. Fledgling emcees clearly saw the marketing potential in battling with others on record.

In 1985, the Juice Crew's MC Shan released "The Bridge" to celebrate his community in Queensbridge, New York. KRS-One took issue with what he perceived to be an incorrect framing of hip-hop's origins on that song. (He possibly used this as an excuse to get back at Juice Crew DJ Mr. Magic for dissing him and one of his earlier tracks.) His group, Boogie Down Productions, responded with the hip-hop history lesson "South Bronx" the next year to set the record straight.

MC Shan came back with "Kill That Noise." BDP's "The Bridge Is Over" followed and summarily ended the battle. One of the greatest and most sampled rap songs of all time, "The Bridge Is Over" is the archetypal hip-hop diss track, an unrelentingly punishing character assassination of the entire Juice Crew. The Bridge Wars helped to put KRS-One on the map, developed the format for rap diss tracks for decades to come, and would inspire Nas, Jay-Z, Tupac, the Notorious B.I.G., and others.

In boxing, they say styles make fights. You couldn't possibly find two rappers who are more diametrically opposed than Drake and Kendrick Lamar: the middle-class Canadian pretty boy versus the diminutive intellectual scrapper from one of America's most notorious hoods. For years, they used each other as boogeymen to fuel their writing. Unbeknownst to the majority of listeners, there was a hidden game of one-upmanship occurring in plain sight between the two of them. And now, here they were face to face, no more subliminal disses, time to go direct.

Wars are often defined by the technology used, and the battle between Kendrick Lamar and Drake has been no different. Arguably the first true rap duel of the internet age, we didn't have to wait months to hear the next diss like during the Bridge Wars. The memes were just as potent as the music, with Drake rumoured to be buying X bots to disparage his rivals. In a short amount of time, we were treated to a cascading fusillade of diss tracks from both parties.

When "Push Ups," Drake's response to "Like That," leaked online in 2024, many initially suspected it was made using AI. The leak appeared to be intentional, a way of testing out public response to the track before officially releasing it, but the rollout felt botched, and it dulled the effectiveness of the strike. "Push Ups" mostly features jabs speculating about Lamar being exploited by his former record label while making fun of his height, the title a reference to a viral video of Kendrick working out. The track was unfocused, with attacks on Rick Ross, Future, Metro Boomin, and others sprinkled in with the disses to Kendrick. This approach would prove to be an arrogant, costly mistake.

Released a few days later to goad Kendrick into responding, "Taylor Made Freestyle" featured Drake dissing Kendrick while using AI voice filters to mimic Tupac and Snoop Dogg over a generic West Coast beat. The title is a reference to Drake's suggestion that Kendrick hadn't yet responded to the previous disses because he was scared to drop with Taylor Swift's *The Tortured Poet's Department* slated for release.

Essentially a futuristic troll job, there was something queasy and distasteful about Drake using Kendrick's hip-hop heroes against him in this way, especially the late Shakur, who has been an idol to Lamar since he was a child. Tupac's estate sent a cease and desist to get the song taken down. The impressions were also clumsy, with Drake's rhyme patterns obvious beneath the altered voices.

One could say this was similar to the various cultural costumes that Drake had readily donned over the span of his career: Caribbean Drake, U.K. Roadman Drake, Latin Drake, the list goes on. It was as if he had tried on so many accents and identities that it became unclear who the real Drake was underneath, an actor after all.

On that misty morning when Kendrick reemerged with "Euphoria," I was reminded of the fact that the most intelligent people often have the deepest capacity for meanness. This song is a laser-focused deconstruction of Drake's essence, painting him as racially confused, a degenerate, a scammer, and a bad father. Kendrick questions whether or not Drake should be allowed to say the N-word, noting that it's cringeworthy whenever he does. There's a biblical fury underpinning Kendrick's bars here, his verses dripping with snarling indignation.

Kendrick does a hilarious impression of the Toronto accent that Drake brought to the mainstream, cleverly using his own cultural impact against him. Lamar's name-dropping of New Ho King has turned the Toronto Chinese restaurant into an international sensation. His strange emphasis on certain words helped turn a few lines into instantly viral moments. A tweaking remark about Drake's braids became a catchphrase for my crew on the rest of our tour.

After landing in Newark ahead of our New York show on the morning of May 3, we were surprised to learn that Kendrick had dropped yet another diss track on Instagram, "6:16 in LA"; on it, he implied that Drake's label had moles who were leaking information to Kendrick's team. At this point, it was as if we were manifesting new diss tracks every time we took a flight. It felt fitting to be in the birthplace of hip-hop for this.

After that song dropped, the battle stopped being about who was the best rapper, rapidly devolving into internecine warfare that made me think worse of both parties. Drake fired back with "Family Matters" later that night, complete with a video where he is seen enjoying a private dinner at New Ho King and a minivan similar to the one pictured on the cover of the deluxe edition of Kendrick's *good kid, m.A.A.d city* gets crushed. Alleging that Kendrick's creative partner Dave Free is the biological father of one of Lamar's kids and that Kendrick has physically abused the mother of his children, "Family Matters" also features some of the most technically accomplished rapping of Drake's career.

In the second section of the song, he effortlessly glides over a fearsome drill track with serpentine flows while dropping the N-bomb twenty-two times in defiance of Kendrick's questioning his racial identity. The third part in particular is a showcase for all the hallmarks of what makes Drake such a successful rapper. Drake lands his funniest line of the whole battle, joking about the Grammys and their propensity for rewarding everything that Kendrick does (now made even more trenchant with Lamar becoming the most awarded rapper in history at the 2026 edition of the awards). A diss track of this magnitude would typically be enough to win a battle, but Kendrick isn't an ordinary adversary.

Before I even knew that "Family Matters" existed, I was already behind. I was out dancing to a DJ set spun by Montréal electronic artist Marie Davidson at Baby's All Right in Williamsburg. I had come directly from my own show at Elsewhere Zone One in Bushwick and had to stuff my merch bag at the coat check when I arrived. Taking a breather in the lobby of the venue, I pulled out my phone and saw a text notification from Josephine featuring the three scariest words that a particular Canadian rapper can imagine: "KENDRICK DROPPED AGAIN."

Less than an hour after Drake had put out his track, Kendrick came back with "Meet the Grahams." It was like dousing a raging fire with a wet blanket. I jetted out of the club and called an Uber immediately. When I got to my sister Gena's place in Harlem, we ordered late-night Chinese food and listened side by side in open-mouthed horror, freaking out after every line. Over a haunting piano beat by the Alchemist, Kendrick calmly addresses every member of Drake's immediate family about what a horrible person he is, ultimately suggesting that Aubrey is hiding an undisclosed daughter.

The great artists show us things that we've never seen before, taking us to places that we can't go ourselves, that maybe we don't even want to go to. This is often in the service of beauty and joy. But "Meet the Grahams" is one of the ugliest songs I've ever heard. It's psychological terror. It sounds evil. It reminds me of watching a *Faces of Death* VHS back when I was a kid, gawking at all the stuff I wasn't supposed to look at but couldn't look away from. I can appreciate how unique "Meet the Grahams" is in the canon of music, but it's not something I'll go out of my way to hear again. Kendrick accuses Drake of running a sex-trafficking ring and being a pedophile, an accusation bolstered by an unearthed clip showing Drake fondling and kissing a seventeen-year-old girl on stage in Denver in May 2010 when he was twenty-three. On the song, Kendrick compares Drake to Harvey Weinstein and says he thinks Drake should die.

The next day during our soundcheck in Silver Spring, Maryland, I saw that Kendrick had followed up that grim entry with the ebullient club banger "Not Like Us." Our sound guy played it over the system, and I knew instantly that Kendrick had beaten Drake with his own "Back to Back" move by making an inescapable party track that doubled as a stinging diss to an adversary. This was a victory lap. I knew that it would spread as rapidly as the virus in M. Night Shyamalan's *The Happening*. Videos of it being played in the club that same night proliferated around the world. People filmed themselves crip-walking to it on TikTok. This was all being done over a diss song that encouraged listeners to keep their little sisters away from Drake.

"Not Like Us" is rich with interpretations, referring to authenticity, culture vultures, West Coast pride, and sexual misconduct allegations against Drake. The lyric about being a colonizer stings in a particularly specific way. Drake literally collects hip-hop memorabilia, some of which used to be the property of his rivals: Pusha T's microphone, Pharrell's chains, Tupac's ring and Death Row chain. It brings to mind the scene from *Black Panther* when Killmonger liberates the African artifacts from the Museum of Great Britain.

In retrospect, the Drake effect seems to have had a vampiric impact on many of the artists who featured him. iLoveMakonnen already had significant street buzz with his mixtape hit "Tuesday" before Drake hopped on the remix and signed him. But after two EPs, a couple mixtapes, and controversy around some uncovered tweets by Makonnen criticizing his label boss, Drake seemingly lost interest and the partnership was dissolved.

BlocBoy JB and others had an initial bump in notoriety after working with Drake that hasn't translated into subsequent stardom. In many of these cases, Drake benefits by gaining street credibility while the artists he works with, especially those he signs, tend to fade into obscurity. And the artists who do manage to become hugely successful after working with him, like Kendrick and the Weeknd, often end up souring on him for unknown reasons.

Looking back on the raging days of this rap war, it feels like an example of what can happen when men have unresolved trauma; they inevitably take it out on others. Kendrick may have won the battle in the court of public opinion, but what did he lose by stooping so low? *Mr. Morale*, his album about the importance of therapy and dealing with trauma, was initially ignored by the masses, and now he's been rewarded with a number one hit in which he gives into his basest impulses.

Both sides weaponized abuse in a post–Me Too world where getting cancelled is the ultimate form of social death. Intimate partner violence, homophobia, and pedophilia were played up for yuks and as gotcha moments. How much more of an appetite do we as a culture have for rap battles where the LGBTQ community, women, and children are collateral damage? The violence spilled into the real world: A few days after "Not Like Us" was released, with artwork featuring a Google Maps screenshot of Drake's Bridle Path mansion with sex offender markers on it, one of Drake's bodyguards was injured in a drive-by shooting there.

A few weeks after the conclusion of my East Coast tour, I hosted a sonics and storytelling workshop back in Toronto as part of the Calling the Conjurers Symposium that was put on by the University of Toronto and Columbia University at It's OK* Studios in May 2024. During the Q&A, a Black academic from the States asked me about "Not Like Us" and what Black identity means in Canada.

Just like we collectively benefitted from Drake's success, Black Canadians newly had to reckon with being seen as colonizers of African-American culture in the weeks after the song was released. Americans online were suddenly pretending that there had never been a Toronto sound in the first place. The idea that we're just tourists and fans with a tenuous and precarious position in hip-hop culture felt like a shadow hanging over us.

It hit differently when you heard Drake's songs in the club in the second half of 2024. In the wake of "Not Like Us," he dropped a new single with Sexyy Red where he rapped over the "BBL Drizzy" meme popularized by his nemesis Metro Boomin. His approach seemed to be to laugh it off and keep things moving. Seeing Drake at the May 23 announcement for Toronto's new WNBA expansion team, I couldn't help hearing Kendrick's disses cycling through my head as I watched him pose for photos with basketball figures.

▶

As time crept by since the turbulent days of the battle, lyrics from Kendrick Lamar's "Euphoria" have only grown more prophetic. The hits were relentless and came from all directions, striking with a razor-sharp intentionality that had never been seen before in a rap battle and likely won't be witnessed again. This is, to date, the only rap battle with a Wikipedia entry that uses the style guide typically reserved for international conflicts.

"Not Like Us" has progressively grown in stature since it first dropped. The cold war between these two had bordered on obsessive; the subterfuge played out like a private game of chess full of jabs and slights likely only noticed by the artists in question. And it was all about to be out in the open with sixteen thousand fans there in person to bathe in the flow of venom.

Notably held on the day celebrating the end of slavery in America known colloquially as Juneteenth, *The Pop Out: Ken & Friends* concert at the Kia Forum in Inglewood, California, was livestreamed on Twitch and Amazon Prime on June 19, 2024. It was a four-hour West Coast rap extravaganza featuring rappers from across California, including a particularly deafening crowd pop for Tyler, the Creator. Kendrick came out to the dulcet strains of "Euphoria" while bathed in flashing crimson beams of light, resplendent in a red hoodie and an uncharacteristically gaudy $750,000 Ben Baller chain with a cross pendant encrusted with invisible princess-cut, 73-carat diamonds. The colour of a Black man's clothing carries added significance and scrutiny in Los Angeles, making red a loaded choice. Kendrick's outfit called back to where he grew up in Compton and also foreshadowed the powerful way this event would end.

His outfit was an homage to what Tupac rocked during his performance of "Out on Bail" at the 1995 Source Awards. It was a significant night for West Coast rap that featured Suge Knight's infamous "Come to Death Row" speech and a frustrated Snoop searching for acceptance from a rowdy New York audience of rappers and industry gatekeepers: "The East Coast ain't got no love for Dr. Dre and Snoop Dogg?" Almost thirty years later, West Coast rap had become central enough to the hip-hop conversation to have a night all to themselves where they could luxuriate in their own regional history. If Drake wanted to pretend to be

Tupac on a record, he would have to deal with Shakur's reincarnation in the flesh.

"DNA," "Element," "Alright," "King Kunta," "Humble," "King's Dead"—bing, bop, boom, boom, boom, bop, bam. Lamar's performance at the Forum was a greatest hits set of songs that subliminally diss Drake.

Lamar carefully highlighted his former labelmates from Top Dawg Entertainment, ceding the spotlight to Jay Rock, ScHoolboy Q, and Ab-Soul throughout his set, contrasting with the increasingly isolated Canadian hitmaker. His mentor Dr. Dre was brought out for "Still D.R.E." and "California Love," leading Dre to ask for a moment of silence before memorably performing the whispered intro to "Not Like Us."

"Not Like Us" was performed five times in a row at *The Pop Out*, recalling Jay-Z and Ye's Watch the Throne Tour where they played "Niggas in Paris" repeatedly every night, including eleven times in a row in the titular city. It's the kind of move that you can only pull when your track has reached a certain level of cultural saturation. With each successive performance of the same track, there is a percolating sense of escalation. How much new life can you squeeze out of familiar material? There was real intention behind Kendrick performing "Not Like Us" exactly five times, seemingly a reference to the number of stocks he mentions he has in the song.

Each performance of the song had a different flavour to it. The first had the maniacal audience shadowing Kendrick's every word like a chorus of ragged ghosts. The telecast featured some inspired, frenetic camera edits during this performance that had the internet going nuts. Ending on the crowd holding the note on "A MINORRRRR," Kendrick paced around the stage like a professional wrestling heel milking the heat from the crowd. "Oh, so y'all ain't gonna let nobody disrespect the West Coast, huh? Oh, y'all ain't gonna let nobody mock and imitate our legends, huh? Let's try it again . . ."

The second time through Kendrick lets the crowd carry almost all of the first verse themselves, the sheer power of their familiarity with the song feeling like a Greek chorus in a tragedy about a fallen king. Lamar hangs again on the "a minor" line. The crowd starts chanting "O-V-hoe" to fill the silence. "One more time . . ." The third rendition is perhaps the most technically accomplished run-through of them all with Kendrick strutting and grooving as he rifles off the vitriol. The final section of the second verse was already one of the most exhilarating moments in music from 2024, but during this performance, it truly felt as if someone turned the knob from simmer to boil on the stovetop. Two dancers emerged, breaking it down with reckless abandon, embodying the crowd's energy.

DJ Mustard returned to the stage. The fourth take starts with just the artist and the song's producer vibing face to face, taking in the spectacle of what they created, a culture-defining moment that will live forever. Former Toronto Raptors superstar and Compton native DeMar DeRozan, wearing an Eazy-E shirt, joins them with fellow NBA icon Russell Westbrook in tow. The stage slowly fills up first with the night's performers and then with an assortment of Black men wearing red and blue.

Kendrick is dapping everyone up as they join the impromptu party. Iconic Los Angeles radio host Big Boy is there, as is Tommy the Clown, the "clowning" dance innovator. It starts to become clear what is happening. "This shit makin' me emotional, man. Fuck that. We been fucked up since Nipsey died!" Kendrick is referring to rap legend Nipsey Hussle, who was murdered in front of his clothing store in 2019. "Let the world see this. You ain't never seen this many sections on one stage keeping it together and having peace." Kendrick then proceeds to organize a group photo with members of rival Los Angeles gangs.

That's the moment when it all became more than just a diss, more than just an argument between rappers. Kendrick took the conflict and used it to galvanize an entire coast. The final performance of the song is pure unbridled Black joy, featuring the unimaginable sight of Crips and Bloods throwing up gang signs and c-walking together. It's also notable for Kendrick's level of comfort in this environment, especially after Drake's weak attempt to question his street bona fides on the first verse of "Family Matters." The end of *The Pop Out* had a rather damning implication: Kendrick is loved enough in Los Angeles to unite the Bloods and Crips, but Drake is too polarizing in his own city to ever try something similar with the gangs of Toronto.

▶

The video for "Not Like Us" was released on Independence Day. Beginning presciently with a shot of the Compton Courthouse, the Dave Free and Kendrick Lamar–directed video is dripping with symbolism. It's a feast of loaded imagery: Kendrick doing push-ups in a jail cell; the recurrent use of red and blue; a handshake in front of shipping containers, appearing to reference human trafficking; a rare appearance from Kendrick's partner, Whitney Alford, crip-walking with their family; an owl in a cage. The video reignited the song's momentum, propelling it to the number one spot on the *Billboard* Hot 100 for the second time.

The calculation behind Kendrick's every move could only be matched by Drake's comparative lack of preparedness. His initial direct response to "Not Like Us" was the ill-conceived "The Heart Part 6," a failed attempt at stealing Lamar's thunder by cribbing the title of what would be the next edition of his "The Heart" series of songs. Subsequently wiped from his Instagram page and never making it to the streaming platforms, it's probably the biggest self-own in hip-hop history. In response to the "Not Like Us" accusations, he bizarrely references Jeffrey Epstein and claims that his fame precluded him from being involved in pedophilia. Huh?

His decision-making in the wake of the beef has defied logic, resembling the desperate actions of a wounded man.

Following this and the Sexyy Red feature, his next post-beef offering was "Wah Gwan Delilah," a collaborative track with Canadian social media comedian Snowd4y. A putrid Toronto patois version of "Hey There Delilah" by Plain White T's, Drake's verse was so questionable that *Billboard* asked two AI detection companies to analyze the song to see if it was really performed by him or not. The results were inconclusive.

"Wah Gwan Delilah" was a curious choice for someone who had recently had his cultural identity and proximity to hip-hop vigorously questioned in front of the whole world, though I have to admit that I'm partial to Snowd4y's verse in which he frantically crams the names of no less than six Canadian banks into one line. Why would Drake make a song like this with a relatively unknown meme artist? Was it hubris? He didn't need the money. Perhaps Drake thought he could joke his way out of it.

All the while, those haunting strings from Mustard's beat must have sounded like the *Psycho* theme to him, and they were everywhere. "Not Like Us" became a cultural phenomenon, going beyond the world of music to influence politics and sports. At press time, it has nearly two billion streams on Spotify. On September 8, it was announced that Kendrick would be playing the Super Bowl halftime show. When J. Cole and Drake bragged about their collaboration being on the same level as the Super Bowl on their war-igniting track "First Person Shooter," they could not have imagined that Lamar would turn around and book the biggest show in the world less than a year later.

Sun Tzu's *The Art of War* dictates that "all warfare is based on deception." It seems clear that Kenny has thumbed through this book once or twice. More than any other musician on this big blue planet, Kendrick Lamar is uniquely capable of "seem[ing] inactive" when he is, in fact, "using [his] forces." It was November 2024, and I was doing my usual listless scroll through the New Music Friday offerings and musing how it seemed to be unusually light on notable releases. Maybe artists were avoiding American Thanksgiving. Or perhaps some industry folks had advance knowledge. Because out of nowhere, the biggest release of them all was finally here. *GNX*, Kendrick's follow-up to 2022's Grammy-winning *Mr. Morale & the Big Steppers*, dropped on November 22, hitting the web like an earthquake. Setting the tone for the album was "wacced out murals" (which was quickly turned into an HBCU marching band arrangement, one of the Blackest things that can happen to a song) with a menacing continuous verse inspired by the vandalization of two Kendrick Lamar murals in LA.

That sense of place is apparent throughout the album, which is distinctively Californian, especially Angeleno. *GNX* is an album that indulges in several of the countless sides of Los Angeles, a prismatic city that will appear completely different to tourists depending on which neighbourhoods they decide to visit. Outside of SZA, who singlehandedly turns "luther" and "gloria" into highlights, Lamar mostly eschews big-name guests for regional artists, many of whom are from opposing LA gangs. This is a statement in and of itself, an album-length representation of the unity photo he organized at his *Pop Out* concert.

Famously teased at the beginning of the "Not Like Us" video, "squabble up" is a squelchy, Debbie Deb–sampling, hyphy banger that evokes Bay Area sideshows. Every reference in the "squabble up" video and throughout the album can function as a rubric for assessing the audience's familiarity with African-American culture. Luther Vandross holds a particularly sacred place for many Black folks, including my family, so the sample of him on "luther" feels poignant and intentional. In light of Drake's ham-fisted AI parody during their battle, Kendrick spectacularly personifies Tupac on "reincarnated" in a pitch-perfect homage that heavily samples Shakur's "Made Niggaz" from the *Gang Related* soundtrack.

That song might hold a key to the album's purpose. "Made Niggaz" is a posse cut featuring the Outlawz. Kendrick's title track similarly finds him ceding the spotlight to a few lesser-known LA emcees: Hitta J3, YoungThreat, and Peysoh. One artist who looms largely over the album but isn't directly shouted out is Drakeo the Ruler, a late Los Angeles rapper known for his idiosyncratic flows who was murdered in a targeted gang attack at an LA music festival in 2021. "Reincarnated" features a conversation between God and the Devil that is reminiscent of DMX's "Damien." Kendrick interpolates "One Mic" by Nas on "man at the garden" and "Kick In the Door" by Notorious B.I.G. on "tv off."

Nothing is done flippantly; there's a crucial subtext to every reference he makes. Rather than behaving like an extractive culture vulture who is demonstrably *not like us*, Kendrick consciously pays homage to the greats all over *GNX*. Nas was notably the only rapper to publicly congratulate Kendrick for getting the Super Bowl halftime show. He's also the guy behind arguably the most potent diss track outside "Not Like Us," one of few hip-hop songs that has become a verb: the withering "Ether" against Jay-Z. It's as if Kendrick is saying, "This is who I relate to. How about you?"

Throughout the album, Kendrick certainly sounds like he's trippin' and he's lovin' it, as he states on the title track. Tapping into his regional roots must feel like a palate cleanser for Lamar, who has built a reputation as the voice of his generation, a Pulitzer Prize winner known for high-minded conceptual efforts. You can feel his looseness on songs like the Super Bowl–ready "tv off," on which he screams producer Mustard's name with such gusto that it became a meme.

The way that Kendrick was interfacing with the public reminded me of how Drake's way around an Instagram caption used to be one of his greatest superpowers. Drake haunts *GNX* as a spectral presence who is merely hinted at but never called out directly, as if to suggest his now-waning relevance.

Days later, Drake broke the hip-hop code by calling for pre-litigation legal action against iHeartMedia and Universal Music Group, accusing them of colluding to promote "Not Like Us." In January, he formally sued UMG, the label he shares with Lamar, for defamation and harassment, accusing it of using bots to inflate the song's streaming numbers. Crucially, these legal actions attempted to dull the impact of a song that was hotter than fish grease. Drake's strategy was to cast doubt on the real-world impact of the track in hopes that he could subsequently change how listeners would hear and perceive it going forward.

One curious wrinkle in how "Not Like Us" was deployed was Kendrick's choice to remove copyright restrictions so streamers on YouTube and TikTok could monetize their reaction videos to the song. When an influencer uses copyrighted music that they don't own in a YouTube video, the sound might get muted, the video could be removed completely, or the advertising revenue could go to the copyright owner. Streamer No Life Shaq celebrated Kendrick for his decision to "think about the reaction community" by allowing them to "eat off this beef" and make "life-changing money" in a video.

A compilation of the best reactions currently has eight point six million views on YouTube. In that collection of clips, their stunned looks and wild dances underline the sheer enormity of "Not Like Us" when it first dropped. This tactic was highlighted in Drake's pre-action petition against UMG, claiming that it "further incentivized influencers to spread the Song," even though it was later disclosed that Drake had also removed copyright strikes for his disses. Several streamers were named in the suit.

His failed efforts were like a Smartcar trying to pull a runaway freight train in the opposite direction. The lawsuits inadvertently gave

"Not Like Us" a fresh shot of outlaw mystique, extending the single's life by highlighting it as the world's most dangerous song. The sheer *not like us*–ness of suing over a rap battle has caused irreparable damage to Drake's image as a hip-hop artist. Joe Budden called him a Karen. Influential radio show *The Breakfast Club* named Drake their "Donkey of the Day" for suing UMG, with Charlamagne tha God saying that by doing so, Drake demonstrates that he "simply doesn't understand culture."

Try to picture Jay-Z suing Nas for untruthfully claiming that he was thirty-six in a karate class. Rap battles have never been about scrupulous fact-checking. It's playing the dozens brought up to the major leagues, yo' mama jokes writ large. Rap battles are a quintessentially Black exercise in gamesmanship, and Drake might now be the pastime's sorest loser ever. There has been a creeping inevitability to Kendrick's song's journey to the top, culminating in Lamar sweeping all five categories that "Not Like Us" was nominated for at the 2025 Grammy Awards.

The award show, which hasn't been attended by Drake since 2019 as a result of his criticism of the institution and subsequent boycott, functioned as an indictment of Drake's place in popular music. As Kendrick repeatedly walked up to collect his trophies, resplendent in a doubtlessly well-considered all-denim ensemble, colloquially known as a Canadian tuxedo, the crowd grew more raucous with each win. In footage of Kendrick sauntering to the stage to accept his Record of the Year award that has since been conspicuously edited and removed from the official Grammys YouTube video (more lawsuits?), you could see Beyoncé clapping and trying gamely to stop herself from rapping along. Taylor Swift is aggressively two-stepping. This crowd of Drake's collaborators, peers, and colleagues suddenly resembled the street celebrations that happen after a despot is overthrown.

And there it was again: the entire audience singing "A MINORRRRR" as soon as Kendrick stepped foot on stage (inspired work by the Grammys production team to use this particular part of the song). There is a gleeful, impish edge to "Not Like Us" that makes the listener feel as if they're doing something they shouldn't be. That rebellious feeling is irresistible, even in rooms beholden to a certain level of decorum. Seemingly, the only person who doesn't like the song is the person being targeted by it.

That man, likely perched on the other side of the world in preparation for his Anita Max Win Tour that started two days later in Australia, must have felt like he was viewing his own wake. When he crooned about the jubilant mood of his eventual funeral on 2022's "Massive," this is certainly not what he had in mind. He opened up his tour in Perth decked out in a black hoodie with bullet holes in it, complete with actual smoke wafting out of the garment, as the beat for "Over My Dead Body" played over the loudspeakers. Subtlety has never been his strong point. Addressing the crowd, he said, "My name is Drake, I started doing music in 2008, I come all the way from Toronto, Canada. The year is now 2025, and no matter what, Drizzy Drake is very much alive." It seemed like the reports of his death were not greatly exaggerated.

When Super Bowl Sunday finally came around, Drake's feeble attempts at halting the march of time and quelling the shifting mores of the music industry were put into sharp relief. No lawsuits or tours could possibly stop this from happening. Kendrick's performance was a love letter to the art of rap, a conceptual tour de force that was unusually thought-provoking for a Super Bowl halftime show. Largely eschewing his hits that were previously performed as a part of the West Coast extravaganza led by Dr. Dre back in 2022, Lamar exhibited impressive bravery and confidence by opening up with an unreleased track and then running through cuts from his recently released *GNX*.

As a rapper, I couldn't help but marvel at the sheer difficulty level of his performance. The cardiovascular endurance required to sprint around, hit his choreography, and comfortably perform these complex verses, all while censoring himself, was an athletic feat, possibly one of the greatest exhibitions of pure rapping ability I've ever seen. Those push-ups really came in handy. I sat in the living room of my friends Lauchie and Shauna, next to a group of wing-eating sports fans who hadn't been monitoring every waking moment of the beef, impressed by what Kendrick decided to pull off on the world's biggest stage.

Starring Samuel L. Jackson as Uncle Sam, Lamar turned his Super Bowl halftime show into a meta commentary on the beef, the loaded expectations around his performance, and the pernicious nature of being Black in America. It was a treatise on "playing the game" that borrowed iconography from the world of video games but functioned more like a Broadway play. When the highly awaited moment to play "Not Like Us" came, it heralded the "a minor" heard around the world. With public repetition, that particular part of the song stopped being only about accusing Drake of something terrible and slowly became vox populi, a barbaric yawp providing communal catharsis.

After the show, we went around the room assessing what we had seen. Opinions were divided. It was an unconventional halftime show. I couldn't focus on what anyone was saying because I was still firmly in Rapper World. It was one of those performances that snuck in during a brief cultural moment when the pendulum had swung further left than it usually does, like when Radiohead performed the uncompromisingly electronic "Idioteque" on *Saturday Night Live* in 2000. Something subversive had broken through the muck again. This was unabashed, unfiltered Blackness in front of 133.5 million viewers who might not have a nuanced perspective on rap music.

Social media takes were initially mixed about the performance with some disappointed by the lack of special guests, muted visual spectacle, and limited colour palette. But like many trail-blazing artistic moments, the performance has steadily gained stature, winning an Emmy for Outstanding

Music Direction. What Kendrick seemed to be saying by keeping the show firmly within his own world is that rap music is enough. It may be hard to remember with Jay-Z's successful run as Super Bowl halftime show co-producer foregrounded in our memories, but there once was a time when a rapper was lucky to be a guest during Maroon 5's Super Bowl set. Kendrick's performance felt like a door opening, a new age beginning.

Five days later, Drake returned with his first full-length effort since the beef, a collaborative album with PARTYNEXTDOOR called *$ome $exy $ongs 4 U*. Clocking in at nearly seventy-four laborious minutes, the boys offer the typically dark R&B-inflected verses that you'd expect from the progenitors of the Toronto sound, providing nothing particularly substantial in the process.

"Nokia" was the comeback hit that he desperately needed post-beef, peaking at the number two spot on the *Billboard* Hot 100. Gone are the pugnacious bars of 2024. Here, Drake cynically digs back into his old bag of tried-and-true tricks to ensure that this single would be a success: the requisite beat switch for TikTok-addled attention spans, shout-outs to the DVP and the 401 to activate his Torontonian audience, and a dance-floor-ready electro beat with an infectious chorus that rifles off the names of various women.

"Gimme a Hug" shows a rare moment of Drake addressing the battle directly, throwing up a white flag by acquiescing to Kendrick's suggestion that Drizzy is better off making club music. The scene painted on "Gimme a Hug" is of Drake returning to the strip club after the lows of the previous year, being greeted with hugs from the dancers like Tony Soprano checking in at the Bada Bing! But you have to wonder what it means for someone to find solace in a place where folks are only your friend if you pay them to hang out with you.

Meanwhile, Kendrick was gearing up for the Grand National Tour with SZA, which started on April 19, 2025. At press time, it had become the highest-grossing co-headlining tour of all time, earning US$254.6 million and selling 1.1 million tickets across twenty-three dates. Drake returned to the stage to successfully headline and curate Wireless Festival in London, where he doubled down on his strong U.K. connections by sharing the stage with Central Cee (who is featured on recent single "Which One"), J Hus, Dave, and Headie One.

Notably, Drake flew in his own press by private jet to cover the shows, including YouTubers and livestreamers like DDG, Adin Ross, BenDaDonnn, and Mississauga's Kyle Forgeard of Nelk Boys, whom Drake also gifted a $150,000, 18-karat yellow gold, diamond-encrusted Rolex Yachtmaster watch for his birthday while they were in London. No one who had posted a favourable reaction video to "Not Like Us" was invited. It's unlikely that anyone who got on the jet will speak negatively about Drake to their massive online followings going forward.

Drake strategically made a point to further ingratiate himself to his British fanbase by saying on stage, "No disrespect to America. No disrespect to my own country. But nobody out-raps London rappers." It is curious that he has rarely performed in North America since the beef exploded in the spring of 2024, beyond a couple guest performances at other artists' Toronto shows. One can see why, with reports of bottles and toilet paper rolls being thrown at him during shows in London and Amsterdam. Can you imagine how a show in Los Angeles would go?

In July, Drake began the rollout for his upcoming album, *Iceman*, with an hour-long livestream. The album title reportedly references the name of an omnipresent Toronto ice delivery company. Drake sat in the break room of their facility and watched early footage of himself on a television that got interrupted by the music video for his album's first single, "What Did I Miss?" In the video, he raps in front of dozens of guns laid out next to a pool at a palatial mansion, presenting an image that is somehow both threatening and nonchalant.

The song itself was less memorable, Drake-by-the-numbers, but the surprise drop netted him a number two debut on the *Billboard* Hot 100. He ended the livestream by driving around downtown Toronto in an ice truck while listening to his own unreleased music as well as the '80s synthpop banger "Spring Is Coming with a Strawberry in the Mouth" by Operating Theatre.

Drake played a new track with Smiley called "2 Mazza" in the truck, which had him shouting out Barrie, Muskoka, Brampton, and Hamilton as if he was campaigning for Ontario premier Doug Ford's spot at Queen's Park. Passersby showed him love along the way, with him eventually getting mobbed by fans at Sankofa Square, Toronto's version of Times Square. Rather than his early regional references, which were inspired by a deep-seated desire to elevate a city and country that had both been long ignored, it was clear that these lyrics and the livestream were part of a larger image-reclamation project to make it seem like he's still the people's champ in his home city. The stream ended with him getting into a confrontation with someone who called him a bitch as he drove by.

In a surprising move, Drake announced that his label OVO would be presenting back-to-back Toronto shows by legendary dancehall artist Vybz Kartel in October 2025, the icon's first-ever performances in the city. An olive branch to the city's Caribbean diaspora, what better way to change the conversation than by being responsible for bringing one of the most beloved Jamaican artists since Bob Marley to Toronto?

After the events of 2024, it's understandable that he would pull out all the stops. What we witnessed over the course of this battle was character assassination on wax on a scale that might not be seen again. One man's reputation is in tatters, both from what was suggested on the tracks and by his own self-inflicted wounds and poor decision-making, while the other successfully wrested control of hip-hop culture away from extractive and colonizing forces, at least for one summer.

Hip-hop discourse has been permanently damaged by this beef, as fans for both sides have become as deeply entrenched in their silos as Democrats and Republicans are in theirs. Other beefs between rappers have happened in the months since the Drake–Kendrick Lamar conflict has died down: Joey Bada$$ against the West Coast, Skepta versus Joyner Lucas. But those tiffs came off as contrived clout-chasing manoeuvres, diss songs as theatre and marketing.

We might have seen the final battle fuelled by genuine hate.

The Age of Anemoia

Mysterious U.K. electronic producer Burial (born William Bevan) is known for his evocative, haunting rave suites tinged with sadness that sound more like the morning after than the heat of the night. Streaked with hiss, video game sound effects, and warped diva vocals, tracks like "Rival Dealer" and "Kindred" can feel like the echoes of proper club tunes with the original source removed, distorted reflections of breakbeat hardcore, jungle, ambient, and U.K. garage that come off like misremembered nights described to a friend over coffee a couple days later.

In a rare 2012 interview with the late Mark Fisher for *The Wire*, Bevan lifted the curtain and shared that his music was inspired by his brother who would go to raves and come back home to share records and stories of his nights out. Burial claimed in the conversation that, at the time of the interview, he'd personally not been to a festival, a rave, or a big warehouse party himself. That's possibly why his songs seem to have a bit of remove to them; they're largely influenced by second-hand memories, tributes to a bygone era that he experienced from a distance.

Also a deconstruction of sounds from the U.K.'s hardcore continuum, Mike Skinner's music as the Streets was a portrait of a London subculture mistranslated by a fan, born in Barnet and raised in Birmingham, into something even more beguiling and compelling. His 2002 debut, *Original Pirate Material*, initially landed on my radar when it was released stateside through *VICE* magazine's VICE Records imprint. Even though I wasn't aware of the complexities of the scene he emerged from back then, there was something strikingly new about this record that pulled me in.

Was it U.K. rap? This guy was no Roots Manuva. The Streets got lumped in with the nascent grime scene when marketed in North America. That classification never quite fit, in my mind. This disconnect was put in sharp relief on the alternate MC mixes of his singles over the years: the "Let's Push Things Forward" remix with Roll Deep in particular makes Mike come off like John Cooper Clarke doing spoken word at a Sunday Roast, especially when paired with a ravenous pre-fame Dizzee Rascal on the same track.

In retrospect, Mike Skinner was just a suburban guy rapping over U.K. garage. U.K. garage is a faster, mutated form of the garage house that dominated clubs in New York and New Jersey in the late '80s and early '90s. Directly inspired by Larry Levan's DJ sets at the Paradise Garage, garage house differed from Chicago house due to the presence of swinging hi-hats, chopped vocal samples, and a more R&B-inflected soulfulness.

In 1993, Timmy Ram Jam and Tuff Jam's Matt Jam Lamont started a club night called Happy Days. If you were to step into the Elephant and Castle pub where this party was held at the absurd hour of ten on Sunday mornings, you'd see DJs taking dub versions of singles by

American artists like Robert Owens and Kerri Chandler and adjusting the pitch control on their turntables to play them at a faster speed for the couple hundred tired ravers coming in after Ministry of Sound had closed for the night next door. Similarly, DJ EZ was pitching up garage house records by New Jersey producer Todd Edwards during his pirate radio show on Freek FM in 1994 to make it more palatable to a British audience used to the breakneck speed of 170-bpm jungle.

Local producers in London started making their own garage tracks, which sounded a bit more unique to their territory, to avoid the expensive import fees on American garage house records. This led to the formation of subgenres like 2-step (a bouncier style without a four on the floor beat that pointed the way toward grime and dubstep) and speed garage (a darker, jungle-influenced derivative style known for time-stretched vocal samples and heavy, sweeping bass) as the '90s rolled on.

Speed garage included some transatlantic flavour with Boston producer Armand Van Helden adding jungle-influenced bass lines to bring the underground sound to the mainstream through his remixes for Sneaker Pimps and Tori Amos. These homegrown British variations eventually settled under the broader umbrella of U.K. garage (UKG) around 2000, the original NYC garage sound transmogrified into an almost unrecognizably different form by the dawn of the new century.

After spending a year in Australia in the late '90s, Mike Skinner returned to the U.K. and moved to Brixton to make an album that he described as being "half hip-hop and half garage." Despite successfully landing a record deal with garage label Locked On for the Streets' debut single "Has It Come to This?," UKG DJs didn't think that the stuff he was making was true garage and were reluctant to play it. That sentiment wouldn't last for long. In a contemporary introduction to a 2000 U.K. garage feature, *The Face* magazine writer Kevin Braddock described Skinner's place in the scene as being "part of it in a rather abstract way—he just seemed to be at the level of street youth culture." Skinner became respected enough by 2001 that you could hear him rapping about geezers wanting to jack his phone on the intro for the fifth edition of DJ EZ's vaunted *Pure Garage* mix series.

Mike Skinner was the sonic representation of the average punter, despite coming from outside London and not hearing the music in its natural habitat. "My experience of garage, which was huge, was in other people's cars and houses, not in clubs," he explained in his 2012 memoir *The Story of the Streets*. "I didn't listen to garage in nightclubs, I listened to it at home." This is the impact of pirate radio: Listeners would tune into unofficial stations that played all the varieties of UKG, grime, and jungle, transmitted from the type of tower blocks pictured on *Original Pirate Material*'s cover.

Mike Skinner clearly wasn't the first person to rap over UKG. But with the Streets, the music was just a little bit different, not as polished and club-ready as the typical 2-step efforts. The occasional R&B hooks by Leo the Lion felt curiously unnatural. And Skinner's voice sounded strange too, wrong somehow. He didn't have the rude boy ragga energy of speed garage vocalists, and he wasn't rhyming with the suave, smooth vibes you'd expect to hear from a 2-step emcee. He didn't rap about champagne or the good life either; his drink was a Kronenbourg. This wasn't MC Neat, Maxwell D, or So Solid Crew. More than anything, he sounded like a character from a Danny Boyle film, a trickster spinning yarns about the minutiae of club culture with a pleasantly surprising, writerly lyrical style.

Even though he was physically removed from the culture, Skinner took his parallel memories and made his own version of what he heard. The twisted results resonated; *Original Pirate Material* was a huge hit, going double platinum in the U.K. and placing forty-sixth, between *Blood on the Tracks* and *Led Zeppelin IV*, on *NME*'s all-time top 100 albums list back in 2003. *The Observer* called him "the voice of Little Britain," a torchbearer for the geezer down the pub who hadn't been heard on this scale since the Happy Mondays, the Stone Roses, or Oasis. And the people were primed to listen.

On "Weak Become Heroes," his magnum opus and, in my opinion, the greatest song about clubbing ever made, we find Skinner reminiscing about his earliest rave experiences. A horny sixteen-year-old taking his first ecstasy pill, young Skinner finds camaraderie in nightlife characters with names like European Bob and euphoria in the sounds of the club environment, as a repetitive piano loop in the song's production functions as a meta-reference.

The third verse zooms forward five years with Skinner sitting in a café, looking back on his clubbing days with lingering ennui. Skinner was only twenty-four years old when this song was released, making this another example of the premature nostalgia that seems to be endemic in young people of his generation. In the outro, Mike curiously shouts out a list of DJs who were synonymous with the Second Summer of Love in 1988 and the U.K.'s acid house craze: Danny Rampling, Nicky Holloway, Johnny Walker, and Paul Oakenfold.

Back then, Skinner would have been ten years old, not exactly an appropriate age for staying up all night at the Haçienda. He follows those shout-outs up by cursing the Criminal Justice and Public Order Act 1994, a piece of anti-rave legislation that went into effect just before or soon after the halcyon teenaged club moment that Skinner memorializes in this song.

The chain of influence continued from the Streets to my own work years later. I was captivated by Mike Skinner's vivid storytelling that depicted the club as a worthy setting and subject, but his disregard for boundaries was also emboldening to me. This was a particularly important inspiration for my sophomore album, *Afterparty Babies*, as well as my collaboration with Jacques Greene called "Night Service." With the lyrics for that song, I was partly influenced by an early tour experience where I played at a club called Avalon in New York City when I was supporting the band Islands.

The venue was a former church that had a history as an infamous nightclub owned by Peter Gatien called the Limelight. It was the real-life club that murderous club kid Michael Alig partied at, as depicted in the movie *Party Monster*. Despite being from Canada and born too late to experience that incarnation of the Limelight, I combined that concept with an allusion to Larry Levan's "Saturday Mass" DJ sets at the Paradise Garage in the chorus. Combing through Tim Lawrence's books about New York's dance music history in the '70s and early '80s, I was often struck by the feeling that I'd been born in the wrong place and was living in the wrong decade. "Night Service" was my way of transporting myself back to that time. Our song explores the spiritual, quasi-religious aspects of club culture, the communion and the reverie, through a historical lens.

"Night Service," Mike Skinner's garage explorations, Burial's rave-evoking productions—they're all examples of anemoia, a particular flavour of nostalgia that involves "a yearning for a past that you never actually experienced," as coined by John Koenig in the *Dictionary of Obscure Sorrows*. It's a close cousin to Jacques Derrida's concept of hauntology as updated by music writers Mark Fisher and Simon Reynolds in the 2000s, described by Dr. David Pattie in *The Oxford Handbook of Music and Virtuality* as "a nostalgia for a future that never came to pass." Anemoia feels unique to people who came of age in the twenty-first century, a time when the present has slowly receded into an ahistorical morass, resulting in a fetishization of what life was like during the more clearly defined decades of the past.

▶

Of all the senses, hearing has by far been the most evocative in my life. Not to knock the joys of brushing hands with your crush or savouring the culinary delights at Joe Beef, but more than anything else, it's been sound that has had the most overwhelming power to transport me. Recently, I saw Theo Parrish play at Standard Time in Toronto. It was early in the night, the room hadn't filled up yet, and he dropped an old favourite of mine. A slow disco pulse poked its head out from the mix in progress, and I identified it as the third song I'd played during my set at the 2018 Red Bull Music Festival in Montréal, one of my fondest DJing memories. The twinkling piano of sensual disco classic "Let's Get Together" by Pam Todd and Love Exchange soared through the air and dragged me onto the just-percolating dance floor.

Our experiences and the people we share them with contribute a richness to music that can be surprising in its longevity and emotional significance. "Ballin'" by Mustard and Roddy Ricch will always remind me of driving around Tehrangeles in Westwood with my wife. Bell Biv Devoe's "Poison" brings me right back to hanging at my grandma's house in West Edmonton with my family during holidays. I'll never forget the moment when a friend was driving me back to my hotel one bleary morning after a Movement Music Festival afterparty in Detroit, and like a needle drop in a movie, she put on "I Want to Be Loved by You" by the Meters, the absolute perfect song for that moment.

There have always been songs that are intentionally nostalgic, that find the artist delving into their past, the songwriting process becoming a therapeutic endeavour. Take Leonard Cohen's "Memories," for example. Produced by girl-group pioneer and future convicted murderer Phil Spector under hostile circumstances, the song finds Cohen looking back on the school dances of his youth. Cohen's lyrical nod to '50s singer

Frankie Laine merged with the song's languorous pace and waltz time signature makes "Memories" a self-referential twirl through the mind's eye, an example of how a nostalgia loop can be formed between songs and their influences.

Hearing certified party starters like D-Train's "You're the One for Me" and "Word Up!" by Cameo can be surprisingly emotional because they're "Teddy records" that I associate with my late father's radio show.

The connections made between music and other media can also be a curiously unique interface. There would be no logical reason to put *Legend of Zelda: Ocarina of Time* in the same sentence as Jay-Z's *Vol. 2... Hard Knock Life*. But they both came out in the fall of 1998, and I played one while listening to the other on Christmas morning as a twelve-year-old. That connection has remained intact after all these years.

Much has been written about music's powerful relationship to memory. Dr. Oliver Sacks famously and perceptively wrote about treating dementia patients by playing songs from their past for them in his seminal book *Musicophilia*:

> Familiar music acts as a sort of Proustian mnemonic, eliciting emotions and associations that had been long forgotten, giving the patient access once again to moods and memories, thoughts and worlds that had seemingly been completely lost. Faces assume expression as the old music is recognized and its emotional power felt. One or two people, perhaps, start to sing along, others join them, and soon the entire group—many of them virtually speechless before—is singing together . . .

Is it possible to be nostalgic for something that you didn't directly experience? The idea reminds me of the timeless koan from Carly Rae Jepsen's "Call Me Maybe," that part where she sings about missing someone before they even came into her life. Even though Nas was only sixteen years old when he wrote the songs that would become his landmark 1994 debut *Illmatic*, there was an outsized sense of reverence for the earliest years of hip-hop all over the record. Introductory track "The Genesis" features a conversation from the 1983 hip-hop film *Wild Style* that leads into a sample of "Subway Theme" by Grand Wizzard Theodore, which was featured in the film.

References to the first wave of hip-hop abound throughout *Illmatic*, particularly curious for someone who certainly would've been too young to go see Grandmaster Flash spin at the Fever or venture from Queens to the Bronx for a DJ Kool Herc block party. Nas was determined to take the listeners on a trip down "Memory Lane," even if the memories were hand-me-downs. On that song, he shouts out the classic 1975 Black coming-of-age film *Cooley High*, which debuted in theatres two years after he was born. Did he watch it on VHS with a family friend while growing up in the Queensbridge housing projects? All this nostalgia mining greatly contributed to Nas's early reputation for being world-weary and wise beyond his years, helping to solidify *Illmatic*'s legendary status in the process.

In a 2014 *XXL* oral history about the making of *Illmatic*, Nas emphasized the significance of carrying the flag for the rappers who came before him out of his borough: "That was a serious weight, representing Queensbridge. I was honored to do it, because of what [MC] Shan and Marley [Marl] had already done." One of Jay-Z's main criticisms of Nas in their battle was directed at his position as a canny observer from his childhood home, peering through the project windows rather than being an active participant in the street stories he rapped about.

But a bit of distance can be a good thing for a writer. Being too immersed in the subject matter can result in bias and a lack of objectivity. It was a crucial difference that Nas rapped about his friends selling crack and not about doing it himself. He was reaching for street credibility by osmosis. Nas's experience is a testament to the nonlinear nature of memory, as his somewhat-indirect nostalgia for early rap and New York urban ephemera inadvertently helped to formalize the tenets of '90s Golden Age hip-hop, setting the standard for all rap records that came after it.

▶

On a YouTube page for Future Sound of London's 1991 rave anthem "Papua New Guinea," the photo used for the video is of an anonymous white-label record on a platter. (Other YouTube videos for electronic tracks even show footage of a pair of hands physically placing a record on a turntable.) A harbinger of mystery, this image is deeply evocative of DJ subculture, the pictured object loaded with intense meaning to clubbers and record-store denizens of a particular age. (This might be why Tame Impala chose to make the artwork for his techno-leaning 2025 single "End of Summer" a stark photograph of a white-label record in a paper sleeve.)

When the audio begins on "Papua New Guinea," you can hear a turntable springing to life for a split second before its cracks and pops give way to the epic ambient breaks of a '90s chillout-room classic. Like countless others across the platform, this YouTube video has become a gathering place for thousands of listeners to wax nostalgic about where a song first found them and where they've gone in life since.

These comment sections are among the most kind-vibed corners of the entire internet. There is rarely any criticism about the track in question, and no insults are hurled between participants. It's a truly safe online space for celebrating music's unique sentimental power. Old and young commingle together, the enterprising raver kids imagining aloud what it might have been like to be in the club when a particular single had first been released. On this particular video, there's a user who reminisces about being "17 yrs old driving around in [their] mk5 ford cortina" in 1992 with the song blasting. There are elegies for "fallen ravers," exhortations to "rave on for all eternity my brothers."

These YouTube comment sections are strikingly similar to virtual guest books for funerals. Except it isn't always a friend of theirs who died; sometimes it's their youth that is being mourned: "We all feel the same don't we? We come hear just for that sweet feeling that takes right back to when life was good. Those parties, these raves, these moments with random strangers in a field at 4am. We really lived back then. I'm grateful for it and i made it out alive," posted @AaronOwenSmith.

Montréal-based filmmaker Mark Slutsky created a Tumblr page in 2012 where he collected the most emotionally resonant YouTube comments that he could find, calling it Sad YouTube. As he explained while discussing the project on Tumblr, Slutsky regularly trawled the hostile currents of an ever-worsening web to pick "amazing nuggets of humanity" out of the detritus, focusing in on those "perfectly crystallized moments of nostalgia and saudade" that might be lost to the sands of time if not for the mechanism of the YouTube comment section.

The results can be surprisingly touching, at times taking on a similar quality to a short story. They are often tales of unrequited love or missed connections. When it comes to memory and music, the songs that soundtrack our lives seem to pair up with loved ones more than with experiences. Commenters treat YouTube like a Ouija board, vainly hoping that their emotional messages might somehow find their way to their dearly departed friends. You can see the different personalities in the typing styles of the users, the grammatical errors and clipped syntax only adding to their humanity. An example from Sad YouTube: "Driving in NYC heading out to the clubs in the early 80's and listening to this. Thinking about the girls that we would run into that night.

Priceless. Hello Gladys from Brooklyn. How can i ever forget you," said @wolf2351 in the comments for "First True Love Affair (Larry Levan Mix)" by Jimmy Ross.

This phenomenon was familiar to music nerds like myself. I had come across posts like this in the past but never realized just how prevalent they were until Slutsky started collecting them. I found this evocative and wistful comment from @dwhite0723 myself recently on a video for the Masters at Work remix of "Buddy X" by Neneh Cherry: "This song put my mind placed in in Fallon Navada around 94. When I was on the military base. I used to run/workout to house cassettes. I remember being on an empty road just jogging and vibing. And it was this MAW exact remix. I wish I could have that time back."

We often like to talk to each other about how music saved our lives or how a song made a significant impact on us. It's a common sentiment. Musicians facilitate the creation of memories, and the songs that live on long past us all are a method of retaining and igniting them. The transformational power of song can come and go quickly, even if the sensation felt potent in the moment. These YouTube comments are a textual record of that spiritual connection, a grasping for the sands of time as they pass through the hourglass, the ephemeral made almost tangible.

It's wonderful that Slutsky documented this style of posting, because it does seem as if it is slowly becoming a thing of the past, a marker of a generational shift. As he points out in a piece about his project that he wrote for *BuzzFeed*, this "accidental oral history of American life over the last 50 years" is an unstable archive with its videos vulnerable to deletion at the whims of copyright holders. With each video that disappears, so do the comments and all the history held within them. Even in the process of writing this, I was unable to track down a comment after finding it earlier in my research, the fugitive post lost in the ether among thousands of others due to Google's unpredictable ranking algorithm.

Some of the Sad YouTube posts were tied to the relatively new wonder of being able to pull up songs on demand. With today's technology, it's practically impossible to not know what you're listening to when you first happen upon it. But in the past, a single would get heard on the radio at random or the listener would have had to wait for the video to come on MTV if they wanted to encounter a given track. This has led to a contemporary genre of user who has finally learned what that song that passed them by was called after decades of searching, posting in the comments to give thanks to the music gods.

Hopping online to reminisce about your past is a type of introspection that doesn't seem to come naturally to younger listeners. That's the territory of TikTok selfie-camera videos and Instagram Live sessions. Outside passionate fandoms like the Swifties and the Beyhive, today's music is not being commented about on YouTube in a way that relates the songs to the listener's previous life experiences. It's possible that one day, listeners may return to the songs of their youth to reminisce about the bygone years in this way, but I wonder if how we use the internet has become less amenable to the self-reflection seen on Sad YouTube. The project was put on hiatus in 2015, and in retrospect, that year feels like a demarcation line for this style of commenting.

Lately, the majority of YouTube comments are directed to the artists themselves, whether it's fans sharing their favourite lyrics or musing about what makes a performer so special. This applies to even the few remaining sentimental posts:

"I'm a contruction worker with a wife and kids. My wife has gone shopping with the girls, my children are out doing their things . . . and here I am, sitting here with the dam surround sound cranked up, subwoofer just a pounding and of all things . . . I got these tears rolling down my unshaven face . . and THAT is the power of Adele," says @tyrone_shoelaces in the comment section for the video for "Send My Love (To Your New Lover)."

On rap videos from the last decade, it's usually just "Who's still here in [insert current year here]?" Possibly a response to the streaming era's rapid proliferation of content, it's as if they're saying that it's surprising when a song is even worth playing again years later, and they hope to explore that amazement with others. "[Random celebrity] brought me here!" is another common refrain. It expresses a desire for community, the post held up as a badge of true fandom, revelling in the charged energy of being around others who arrived somewhere for the same reason as you. There are plentiful references to memes and tons of kids trying to get jokes off, as humour has supplanted vulnerability online in the era of the troll.

Perhaps the dearth of relatable human comments could be due to the rise of bots on social media. A 2025 study by Lynnette Hui Xian Ng and Kathleen M. Carley called "A Global Comparison of Social Media Bot and Human Characteristics" found that an average of 21.9 percent of X users commenting on a variety of topics were bots. The number climbs to 43.9 percent for posts during the 2020 U.S. presidential election. According to Imperva's 2025 "Bad Bot Report," there are now more bots than humans online for the first time in a decade with automated activity accounting for 51 percent of all web traffic.

While a future where the internet is solely populated by bots holding conversations with each other as prophesied by the dead internet theory is unlikely, the prevalence of AI-generated comments on social media has certainly made being online a lot less fun. And that doesn't even take into account the malicious bots who intentionally mislead the public during elections. Just take a look at any successful engagement-bait post that prompts users to share a personal story, and you'll see the glimmering light of humanity sparkling through the screen—our wins, foibles, idiosyncrasies, and recollections still charmingly impossible to replicate.

▶

In 2023, Kleigh Balugo asked a question in *Dazed* that had been on my mind for some time: "Why have people looked the same for the last 20 years?" The author points out that "aesthetic differences between the '60s and the '80s, or the '70s and the '90s, are so strong that you can tell what time period a movie is set in based solely on what someone is wearing." But the differences are nowhere near as stark when looking only at the twenty-first century.

The last two dominant aesthetic movements that were somewhat unique to their time were electroclash (early 2000s) and indie sleaze (late 2000s), and it's a sign of the times that indie sleaze has been largely defined retrospectively through the Instagram page of the same name. But even those eras were openly derivative of the past, particularly drawing on looks and sounds from the '80s new wave and '70s rock scenes respectively.

The Patterning's Patrick Metzger wrote about the concept of the thirty-year "nostalgia pendulum," where "it takes about 30 years for a critical mass of people who were *consumers* of culture when they were young to become the *creators* of culture in their adulthood," resulting in a resurgence of old intellectual property in film and TV as well as the marketing of our youths back to us as adults. I would argue that the unique circumstances of our time are shortening the cycle to around twenty-five years, which lines up perfectly with the late '90s and early '00s nostalgia that feels particularly prevalent halfway through the '20s.

Beyond nostalgia cycles, there is also a general aesthetic flattening that has newly reared its head. I remember back when *VICE*'s style report highlighted different folks from around the world to represent how people dressed in those cities. It would be illuminating. "Wow, I didn't know Copenhagen was rocking like that," I'd say. When I watch street fashion YouTube channels today, from Paris to New York to Toronto, there is a striking homogeneity to what people are wearing that wasn't present even two decades ago.

This has also gone hand in hand with a visible decline in people basing their aesthetic on a particular subculture. You used to see people walking down the street and easily be able to identify them as a punk, a goth, a hip-hopper, a metalhead, or a raver. If you were part of one of those scenes, how you dressed was a shorthand way of building community, announcing yourself as part of a group before you even said a word. With the exception of the rise of the drag scene, a person publicly aligning themselves with a specific subculture has become rare in recent years.

In an essay for *Far Out* magazine called "A Farewell to Subculture: The Death of Belonging," Tom Leatham wrote that a subculture is defined as "a group of people whose beliefs are opposed to those of broader society." The piece suggests that there is now "less distinction between what's considered the belief and aesthetic of the wider cultural group and that which deviates from it," rendering the subculture as we once knew it effectively obsolete. Those well-defined groups have been replaced by hyper-individualism spurred on by social media, where younger generations mix and match cultural signifiers seemingly at random with no regard for their original context.

Social media has placed us in an interminable state of the forever present—life in the form of a grid—where we've all become loathe to puncture our public image with evidence of a brief detour, when for a year we were a steampunk or whatever. While some might say that these subculture scenes now exist online, such as with the e-girl aesthetic, Leatham criticizes social media by saying that it's become too easy to "assimilate the mere aesthetic of a subculture without doing any of the hard work." That's how we've ended up with online identities that feel flimsier, less definitive, and more fragmented than the alternative subcultures that broke through in the '90s.

One of the last vestiges of the hipster subculture is their meta-referential desire to flaunt their individuality by drawing from bygone fashions and media. I'm not immune to this impulse myself. I recently bought a vintage 1992 Pentax Espio 70 point-and-shoot film camera to cut down on how much I pull out my iPhone 14 Pro and to give my social media posts a more organic feel. I even went so far as to start a vintage clothing reselling venture called Searcher Vintage where I curated a selection of preppy '90s fashion.

Part of that experience was linked to an appreciation for the higher-quality natural materials of the past, which have been replaced with cheaper synthetic alternatives. My personal thrifting has found me unconsciously targeting totems of the early 2000s, such as the 2001 Nike Triax C3 watch I snagged recently. Its curvy, futuristic shape and appealing lack of smart functionality unexpectedly inspired me to search for electronic music from the same time period.

I've grown attracted to the ambiguity in the production of club music from around the turn of the century, pleased by how polished, ultra-modern, and clean it sounds while still retaining the organic, occasionally analog production methods common before the democratization of computer technology hit near the middle of the '00s. It's somewhat similar to the period between 1979 and the mid-'80s when analog recording had reached a technical apex and digital recording had not yet become the standard.

When the music that I'm talking about first came out, it wasn't on my wavelength. I was there, but I wasn't there. I mostly listened to underground rap back then. I obtained most of my hip-hop knowledge from print magazines. This was the era of the 56k modem; you couldn't quickly do a crash course on a music scene in a day or two like you can now. Perhaps this is what has my generation feeling anemoia today: Even for the stuff that we were ostensibly around for, our present lack of a well-defined decade has motivated us to go time-travelling.

Clipse, Playboi Carti, and Tyler, the Creator have included DJs screaming over their tracks on recent albums as a callback to the mixtape era of the late 2000s. There was once a time when these interjections were considered a nuisance by many listeners; now they have become hallmarks of authenticity and cultural history. Once a ruthlessly nihilistic subgenre whose rappers were seemingly immune to waxing nostalgic, time has made even the hardest trap stars go sentimental.

Hosted by DJ Spinz, Metro Boomin's newest release *Metro Boomin Presents: A Futuristic Summa* is the trap mixtape equivalent of a shot-for-shot film remake. Bringing back Atlanta mixtape rappers who reached their heights of fame in the 2010s, like Travis Porter, Roscoe Dash, Waka Flocka Flame, and Young Dro, the tape comes off like an attempt to reclaim trap's origins in the light of the genre's rapid international journey and subsequent appropriation over the past couple decades.

Recently, my friend Sarah started taking selfies while sitting in her car for her Instagram story. In each of these effortlessly aesthetic photos, she was holding up a relic of the past, an emblem so inescapably tied to the '90s that most people don't even have a way to use them anymore: a compact disc. Bought out of necessity, since she was driving a car old enough to still be equipped with a CD player, the anachronistic was suddenly chic again. First it was just one at a time. Then she posted a haul of discs she'd found in a single day of thrifting, carefully arranged on the passenger seat: two Rihanna CDs, Lana Del Rey's *Born to Die*, *Merriweather Post Pavilion* by Animal Collective, the Knife's *Shaking the Habitual*, *Kala* by M.I.A. It could've easily been a photo from a decade ago.

My renewed interest in electronic singles from the late '90s and early '00s has lined up nicely with a contemporary resurgence of speed garage and U.K. garage worldwide. Artists like Conducta, Interplanetary Criminal, Oppidan, and Sammy Virji have brought the sound back to prominence after a couple decades out of the spotlight. And once considered to be an outlier, Mike Skinner is now seen as an elder statesman in the UKG scene. U.K. garage has become the perfect soundtrack for our cultural moment: fast, futuristic, and nostalgic all at once.

Now we get to have a do-over—we can relive the '90s as the person that we are today. Or we can watch, wear, and listen to what we would have been had we lived in Manhattan in the '70s. Maybe it's all escapism, a trauma response to a pandemic, a genocide, and a global turn to the hard right politically. We aren't the first generations to have curiosity about what came before us. But we are the first to have the technology to turn our longing into reality.

Taking the Scenic Route

In December 2023, Spotify laid off over 1,500 employees (17 percent of its staff at the time) before the holidays, including human playlist curators. Earlier that year, it had launched an ad for a product that could function as their replacement.

A hip-looking young man in a well-appointed apartment sits in a leather computer chair and slides on a pair of silver headphones. The most faceless music known to man is playing in the background, a sort of beachside disco soundtrack composed by androids who led uneventful lives. The man pulls out his phone, and a luminescent Spotify logo is staring back at him from the screen. He clicks a button, and a voice speaks to him using his name, promising a shocking new innovation: Spotify will now provide him with his own personal AI DJ.

The ad received widespread mockery across social media. As is common with most AI integrations, it is a product that literally no one asked for that has been aggressively foisted on an existing audience. What

Spotify's AI DJ actually does involves a pale imitation of a cool person (voiced by Spotify's head of cultural partnerships Xavier "X" Jernigan) that crudely crossfades between songs you've liked in the past, tracks you've listened to recently, and some algorithmic suggestions based on your historical listening data.

As I write this, the droid behind the decks has just switched from a languid '80s Brazilian funk tune by Jorge Ben that I was really into a month ago to a high-paced, U.K.-garage-tinged remix of Coco & Clair Clair by the 1975's George Daniel; it's a jarring, breakneck transition that no real person would ever willingly attempt. And then Jernigan's disembodied voice reappears to take a stab at music journalism, introducing the next track by clumsily juxtaposing the techno pop of Kelly Lee Owens with the work of chameleonic cello pop iconoclast Arthur Russell in a weirdly imprecise comparison.

The AI DJ's puerile observations are as inane as they are disturbing. A more uninitiated listener might take the machine's statements at face value, perhaps causing a young person to carry wrong-headed observations with them for the rest of their lives into real-world conversations with their peers. It reminds me of when Google AI informed me that Dirk Nowitzki was still an active NBA player. As companies have rushed to embrace AI technology, we've been forced to trade accuracy for expediency, clarity for convenience.

It seems as if Spotify's AI DJ is its answer to internet radio stations like NTS that tap music curators, DJs, and artists from around the world to share their well-considered sonic favourites, but the user experience on these platforms couldn't be more different. Unlike a great DJ mix, using Spotify's DJ feature is often frantic and stressful. Spotify's DJ is a gross oversimplification of what a real selector actually does. DJs aren't just people who stand behind a table and press Play. When a real DJ gets behind the decks, they step into the booth with decades of experience and situational awareness that has been fine-tuned and sharpened by countless sublime and miserable gigs. Their skills have been directly informed by their journey.

One such selector is Flo Dill, the affable longtime host of *The NTS Breakfast Show*. Listening to her charming broadcasts, you're destined to hear something unique that will stick with you. Flo is a fount of knowledge, and I often learn something new when I tune into her show. I consider myself to be a massive music nerd, so I'm routinely shocked when I hear her slot in a song that I thought was just my little secret. No genre is safe from her purview, and her passion for music of all kinds knows no bounds. But Flo never comes off like a gatekeeper in the process, speaking between tracks with a warm-hearted, joyful exuberance that belies the subtle mastery of her curation.

Legendary Detroit-based producer and former NTS resident Theo Parrish's epic, soulful DJ sets generate a crowd response that verges on the ecclesiastical. He careens into mixes that most DJs wouldn't dare attempt, some of which find the transitions teetering on the edge of collapse, Parrish balancing the decks like a plate-spinning circus act. Having seen him multiple times in three different cities and read interviews about his life, I know there can be a memoiristic quality to his selections. The deeply personal tenor of his record choices makes him impervious to impersonation. His crates are well-earned, equally informed by his journeys around the globe as well as by his time tethered to the birthplaces of house and techno, Chicago and Detroit.

His *Ugly Edits* series is a showcase for his inimitable talent for pulling the rug out from underneath an existing song. Parrish's sensuous re-edit of "Slowly Surely" by Jill Scott finds his patient hand incrementally shifting the tectonic plates beneath what was once a typical neo-soul track, as if he were J Dilla in slow motion. AI would likely struggle to generate a playlist that truly captures the nuances of his playing style. I've gone back and listened to individual songs in the glow of the next day's morning light, and they somehow don't sound the same as they did coming out of his mixer during his set the night before.

Maybe it was an edit; maybe it was played at a different speed. Or perhaps it was the context in which he played the songs, the reasons why, the meaning ascribed to it all, that made it sound completely different. Equally interesting is what happens whenever I play songs that I've heard in other people's sets, and they don't hit the same when I spin them. They can feel like ill-fitting hand-me-downs on a child, the clothes wearing the wearer. Without the original context, it's merely a performance, a replication of someone else's experience. This isn't necessarily a bad thing though. Mimicry is but a rest stop on the road to individual style. And with time and exposure, those songs are folded into my collection as I build a closer relationship with them.

Spotify's DJ can only offer you more of what you already like, rarely straying beyond the guard rails of the taste profile you've previously established. DJs like Flo and Parrish guide you toward what you didn't even know you needed. The AI DJ is a rote song-delivery system bringing your favourites to your door just like Postmates. While NTS has its problems—there are questions about the station's future direction in light of Universal Music Group acquiring a 49 percent ownership stake—listening to a mix on an internet radio station is still one of the most genuine methods for authentic song discovery out there. Hearing something that stops you in your tracks, a song that makes you question how you could have spent your entire existence up to that point without it, can be life-altering.

You won't have to look much further than a 2025 Spotify app update to get an idea of how the tech giant plans to further integrate AI into its service. Users were furious when the Library button was replaced with a Create button on the mobile app, a UX choice clearly made to take advantage of muscle memory. When erroneously clicked, it brings up a menu with different playlist creation options.

Marked with a green Beta tag is an option titled AI Playlist. "Your playlist playground awaits," declares a title card when you click, and there's a text box where you can enter a prompt. My request for "U.K. garage for main stage at a summer festival" generated a playlist called U.K. Garage Festival Vibes that skewed a little too mainstream for my tastes. My attempt to refine the prompt by adding "Jamaican rasta vocals" failed to improve the results. As flawed as they might be, these are all cuddlier use cases for AI than former Spotify CEO Daniel Ek's much-maligned €600 million investment in AI military drone company Helsing.

▶

During the rollout for my 2024 album *Rollercoaster*, I found myself being interviewed by reporters from the tech sector. That record critically examined the social media era while also functioning as a love letter to the early internet. Vass Bednar from the *Globe and Mail* had me on the podcast *Lately* in June of that year. It was a collegial, wide-reaching conversation about my experiences as an artist in the algorithmic era and how it differed from when I first came on the Canadian music scene in the early '00s. Near the end of our chat, Vass presented me with a surprise: Their team had prompted Suno AI to make a theme song for their show in the style of my music as Cadence Weapon. Did I want to hear it? I responded with nervous laughter, but I was game to check out what it had come up with.

Some musicians might've been offended by this gag. Artificial intelligence has been seen as an existential threat to artists ever since the advent of apps like ChatGPT and Suno. If what they played was a close copy, I might have felt threatened. Fortunately, what the app came up with was a grotesque, superficial interpretation of my music that seemed trained solely on *Rollercoaster* and hadn't considered any of the albums I'd made before. The theme song featured an up-tempo boilerplate electro beat with fake guitar and some vaguely edgy rhyming lyrics performed lifelessly. It sounded a bit like a Linkin Park parody and not much like my music. It was unremittingly terrible. It used the slang term *cray*. But if you were to ask a tech evangelist, they'd probably say it was curtains for me.

That's the interesting thing about the conversations we've been having about AI since these tools began attempting to simplify artistic processes for the masses. No matter how devoid of the glimmering spark that separates humanity from machine this AI slop is, there's always some tech fanboy waiting in the wings, ready to declare victory over us pretentious artists. Though it's undeniable that previous technological innovations opened doors to a wider spectrum of potential artists, I have to laugh at the idea that these AI apps are newly democratizing music by making it easier for anyone to create. What you generate with an AI app like Suno is not music; it's a parlour trick. Other than a quick chuckle from someone initially amazed by the process, there is no inherent value in what is produced with this technology.

That hasn't stopped some professional musicians from adding AI to their workflow. A few months ago, I was sitting in a producer's home studio with top-of-the-line equipment all around us. He'd had some significant placements on albums by big-name artists. There was all the bric-a-brac that you might expect to see in a music studio, including charming drawings by his kids. Usually, a recording session involves bouncing ideas off each other to make a song piece by piece. But during this particular session, the producer started things off by loading up an AI app that generated a drum loop for him to start his beat with.

I was gobsmacked. It was a dusty boom-bap-drum pattern with all the veneer, swing, and character of a classic hip-hop beat. It was pretty convincing. He eventually played guitar over the loop and replaced what the technology had spit out with his own drum sounds. But I still sat there with a sour feeling. It harshed the vibes of the entire session for me. I couldn't help but be stunned by his laziness. "Bro, your job description is *beatmaker*," I thought. Making a beat is literally the whole point of being a producer, and he didn't even do that.

Drum machines can be played and mastered just like any other instrument, even when electronic samples are used. No one would deny the skill required to manipulate an MPC the way that DJ Premier does. Even electronic drum programming with a digital audio workstation on a laptop can clearly convey the personal style of the producer who tapped the beat in. What the producer I worked with did was ask AI to fabricate unique rhythmic qualities and sonic flavour from what was likely a previously existing classic hip-hop breakbeat, instead of laying down his own sonic fingerprint.

It made me think about how he got to that point. I imagined the joy and excitement he must have felt back in the day, listening to the legends of hip-hop make magic with drum machines, samples, and synthesizers, using their hands to craft the vibrant soundscapes that would shape our lives. Why, decades later, as a jaded professional, had he opted to forgo that process and let a line of code do it for him? I was watching someone make themselves obsolete. I wondered if relying on this tool had made him less driven and inspired elsewhere in his career. I left the session early. The demo he sent back only had my verse and some melodic wordless mumbling by him. He asked me if I had any ideas for what he should sing about. The song was never completed.

There has been much hand-wringing about where the line is for acceptable AI use in music. Landr is a company that uses AI to mix and master tracks, providing a cheaper option for neophyte musicians. Some consider the pitch correction technology of Auto-Tune, one of the most used plugins in popular music, to be a form of AI. Serato Stems has revolutionized production and DJing by making it possible to take any song and separate it into individual parts. It was once only possible to get stems through privileged access to official studio masters, but now there are several consumer apps with access to this technology.

It's true that some artists use AI in their creative process as just another tool in their arsenal. In 2023, patten released an album called *Mirage FM*—the first record to be made entirely from samples created using AI prompts. The result is a suite of vaporous dreamlike sound collages that hint at the lo-fi beat scene, complete with vocal chops of a wordless non-language that sound like a machine's interpretation of soul singing. Listening to the album felt like driving from town to town and getting stuck between competing radio frequencies. The songs float around wraithlike, an inert assemblage of sonic signifiers harshly groping for meaning and melody where none can be found, making the record a prime example of how AI art often values process over result.

AI has found a controversial place in the world of hip-hop, a genre known for skirting the lines of legality in its quest for the perfect beat. As mentioned previously, Metro Boomin sampled an AI-generated soul track called "BBL Drizzy" while quarrelling with Drake, turning it into a viral sensation by offering $10,000 and a free beat to the person with the best verse over his track. For "Either On or Off the Drugs," JPEGMAFIA sampled a cover of Future's "Turn On the Lights" by AI for the Culture, which takes an Atlanta trap classic and reimagines it as a '70s R&B slow jam. Rather than coming off as a stunt, JPEG's use of AI feels like a creative decision in line with his usual boundary-pushing production choices.

Ye has been a major proponent of AI use as a means to replace his own voice on his songs. Already well-known for getting other rappers to create reference tracks with ghostwritten lyrics that he later uses to make the final verses on completed recordings, he's made the process more streamlined by having other people rap reference verses while using a Ye AI voice filter and then just leaving that in the song. His horrified fans have taken to calling him Ye-I on Reddit.

After years of adding more and more collaborators, producers, and songwriting camps to his process with each successive album, we've now reached a point where Ye has become a guest on his own records. Unlike the aforementioned examples of producers who used AI as a starting point for further creativity, Ye uses AI as a means for putting even less effort into his music, creating increasingly soulless output.

Like during the NFT craze, a number of celebrities have hitched their wagons to the AI boom. While promoting his new digital book, *The Way of Code: The Timeless Art of Vibe Coding*, on an episode of *The Ben & Marc Show* podcast, Rick Rubin called AI "the punk rock of coding," sharing optimism around its democratizing qualities. Timbaland recently launched Stage Zero, an AI entertainment company, and his flagship artist TaTa is a young pink-haired female digital pop star with a K-pop aesthetic, whom he describes as being "a living, learning, autonomous music artist built with AI." TaTa's music is generated by Suno.

Producers like Rubin and Timbaland are already established, insulated by their wealth and fame, and they both have a financial stake in the success of the technology. From the comfort of their long careers built during more stable times for the music industry, they don't have to worry about the impact of having their own tracks scraped by AI the way that emerging artists do. It's also likely no coincidence that AI seems to be particularly appealing to older figures who are far removed from the most fruitful creative periods of their careers.

Timbaland admitted as much in a March 2025 interview for *Rolling Stone*. "I thought it was over," he confessed to Brian Hiatt from the studio in his Miami mansion. "Music is a young sport. I am the best, right? One of the best producers ever. I can make the drums, but something about it don't hit the same way in this generation." Referring to Suno as "Baby Timbo" and "my *Thriller*," he claimed to have made "a thousand beats in three months" culled from "more than 50,000 song generations" that he created using the app. (*Thriller* was the high point of an already illustrious career for Quincy Jones, so this suggests that Timbaland believes that Suno will provide him with a similar career boost during a down period for him. *Thriller* has become shorthand for "most successful album of all time." It is still the best-selling album in history.)

An AI-generated teaser video for a pair of TaTa songs was shared on Timbaland's TikTok account in July 2025. Featuring a futuristic Asian theme reminiscent of the timeless *Crouching Tiger, Hidden Dragon*–inspired, Dave Meyers–directed clip for Missy Elliott's "Get Ur Freak On," one of Timbaland's biggest hits, the music in the AI video is bland radio R&B that lacks the edge and curiosity of classic Timbo. In the AI song, TaTa sings about checking her pulse. One can't help but compare it to his unforgettable work with a flesh-and-blood human woman: the late Aaliyah. TaTa feels like a strange replacement for arguably his greatest creative partner who left us too soon, a stand-in who is impervious to the vagaries of fate.

On beats like Missy and Ludacris's "One Minute Man," you can literally hear Timbaland's tireless creativity as the track rolls on. Chopping a guitar intro from singer-songwriter David Pomeranz's "Greyhound Mary" and bathing it in chirping acidic synths, he gestured toward several genres at once, but the song remained excitingly indefinable. At his peak, Timbaland took source material and created something otherworldly with it; his use was always transformative. The beat's outro introduces a fresh countermelody that might have been enough to carry an entire other song. His habit of shocking us with these new parts to close out his songs made him seem like a restless kid who wasn't ready to stop playing at the park.

The story of TaTa reminds me of the furor around FN Meka, the "virtual rapper" unveiled in 2022 and subsequently dropped by Capitol Records after it was uncovered that white programmers at Factory New were behind the Black-presenting digital avatar who arrived with green dreads and face tattoos. Dropping N-bombs and rapping about police brutality, he looked like a SoundCloud rapper straight out of central casting. Civil rights groups condemned FN Meka, likening it to digital blackface. Factory New hired a Black emcee named Kyle the Hooligan to come up with FN Meka's rhymes and then allegedly never paid him for them. The experiment was a total mess, dead on arrival.

But AI was less robust back then, requiring more tricks behind the curtain. Human listeners are naturally resistant to the uncanny nature of AI music. But in the case of the Velvet Sundown, technology had improved enough to fool people into listening. There was much consternation about whether or not this country-fried rock band that had amassed 900,000 monthly listeners on Spotify was real. Garnering a cavalcade of press from all corners of the media world that any real human band would dream of, the shadowy figures behind the Velvet Sundown pretended to be authentic until they eventually amended their Spotify bio to admit that they were "a synthetic music project guided by human creative direction, and composed, voiced, and visualized with the support of artificial intelligence."

Part of their initial buzz was derived from the fact that listeners were streaming their music in droves. The Velvet Sundown somehow managed to get on a Spotify playlist of dubious provenance called Vietnam War Music that had 647,212 followers. But they didn't actually fight in or protest the war, making their placement on such a playlist the virtual equivalent of stolen valour. Songs like "Dust on the Wind" deal in hollow anti-war platitudes that lack the emotional poignancy and lived experience of the human bands who actually survived the tumultuous '60s, risking their careers and sometimes their lives to speak truth to power.

Lucas Woodland of Welsh emo-rock group Holding Absence took to X to sound the alarm about an AI artist called Bleeding Verse that had cited his band as an "influence" on its YouTube channel bio, which seemed like a euphemism for training the AI on their music. Insinuating themselves onto user's algorithmic playlists, Bleeding Verse was able to surpass Holding Absence, a band that had been around since 2015, in monthly listeners on Spotify after only two months.

It's impossible to know how many bots were involved in making either of these groups appear to be successful bands. A former Spotify "data alchemist" told *Rolling Stone* that the Velvet Sundown's popularity may be thanks to paying Spotify for preferential playlist placement, or because the app's algorithmic recommendation system organically picked up on the group's characteristics and sent their music out to users like any other band. After the initial media attention, the Velvet Sundown's monthly Spotify listeners shrunk to just over 160,000. By the time this is published, it'll likely be even lower.

A new technique for companies attempting to normalize the use of artificial intelligence in entertainment industries is by building buzz that an AI-generated artist is talented enough to be worthy of significant investment. During a panel at the 2025 Zurich Film Festival, Eline Van Der Velden, founder of AI production studio Particle 6, disclosed that their AI actress Tilly Norwood has allegedly "attracted the attention of multiple talent agents." After racking up millions of streams, AI R&B act Xania Monet and the Mississippi poet Telisha Jones who writes her lyrics reportedly signed a multimillion-dollar record deal with Hallwood Media, an indie label started by former Interscope executive Neil Jacobson.

AI artists like these feel like trial balloons for the public's tolerance for generative music, a way of selling songs without the musicians.

But the gambit will only work if an AI artist actually makes something that can hold up to criticism and stand the test of time. This has yet to happen.

Stage Zero co-founder Rocky Mudaliar told *Rolling Stone* that Timbaland was hoping to "pioneer a new genre of music—A-pop, artificial pop." But Timbaland was already a trailblazer. It's sad to picture one of the most groundbreaking hitmakers of his generation, the innovative mastermind who defined the 2000s through his singularly iconic beats for Jay-Z, Justin Timberlake, and others, and who inspired countless artists across all genres in the process, being so bereft of ideas that he has to plop in front of a computer and pray that an AI can help him get his swagger back.

After being identified as a "power user" of the platform, Timbaland was named strategic advisor at Suno, putting him in charge of "creative direction" and "day-to-day product development." In an interview with *Rolling Stone* about his appointment, he called Suno "the best tool of the future" that "allows you to get any idea in your imagination out of your head." In June 2025, Timbaland got torched online for lifting a beat by K Fresh without his consent and feeding it into Suno to make a new track in a video.

The older generation of musicians has a boomer-ish fascination with AI that might be kind of endearing if not for the grim implications around much of it. Rod Stewart was under fire for projecting an AI tribute to fallen artists on a screen during a performance of "Forever Young" in Alpharetta, Georgia, at the Ameris Bank Amphitheatre. In the video montage, the recently deceased Ozzy Osbourne was seen using a selfie stick to take mugging photos in the clouds alongside a motley crew of superstars so random that I simply must name them all: Tina Turner, Bob Marley, Tupac Shakur, Michael Jackson, Freddie Mercury, George Michael, Amy Winehouse, Aaliyah, Prince, Kurt Cobain, Whitney Houston, and XXXTentacion.

Was Ozzy actually friends with any of these artists? Had he ever even used a selfie stick? This dystopian, necromantic fan fiction was Stewart's way of paying homage to artists who had passed away using some gee-whiz new technology. He likely had good intentions, but it came off like *Weekend at Bernie's*, distastefully dragging some corpses around for entertainment. The worst part was the grotesque and unnaturally open-mouthed smiles on their faces. The stars look as if they're trapped in some sort of virtual purgatory. Behind their eyes, they're screaming for our help.

▶

After the *Globe and Mail* podcast experience, I decided to try my own experiment. I fed ChatGPT all the lyrics from my album *Rollercoaster* and asked it to write a synopsis. I was somewhat surprised by the observations made by the AI. Regarding my song "Blue Screen," the app said, "The chorus 'Crashing again' could refer to the experience of computer crashes, but also seems to suggest a feeling of emotional or mental collapse." I hadn't intentionally made that particular connection when I wrote the song. It's likely that I would have come to the same conclusion talking about the track to a human friend, but I have to admit that the app saw my song from a new perspective.

Some of the best applications for ChatGPT are summarizing and gathering information. I prompted the AI to search for italo disco songs from 1984 similar to "Dancing Shoes" by Pancho Ballet. Italo disco is a subgenre of dance music originating in Italy that was popularized in the '80s and enjoyed a resurgence in the '00s. Think of it as the missing link between '70s disco and '80s synthpop. A plaintive electro-pop ballad that is melodramatic in its almost pathetic level of yearning, "Dancing Shoes" stays just on the right side of the cheesy–amazing binary that governs the world of italo disco. The singers belt out the song's overwrought lyrics with a misplaced intensity that is charming in its earnestness. The double-tracked vocals and high-octave singing seem to be influenced by the Bee Gees, the brotherly boy band that ruled the mainstream disco era in the '70s.

Like with many other italo songs, the words appear to have been crudely translated from Italian to English. They sing about their love interest knowing how to dance, but they lost their dancing shoes. We vaguely get what they mean here—it's a romantic metaphor grounded in a dance club. But the garbled translation is what gives it the emotional juice. These quirked-up exhortations tap into some animal sense of longing that we all have preprogrammed inside us. Putting it logically would only get in the way. The narrator sings about his dance partner having no shoes in such a pained manner that it sounds as if his tears are practically dripping on to the microphone. We want to learn how to help them find their kicks.

This blend of charming naïveté, emotional heft, and addictive tunefulness can be hard to find in the genre, especially all on the same song. I've cultivated my crate of tracks that carry this feeling over many years, building it through the organic means of digging online and in person at record stores. I've spent hours on Discogs, manipulating search terms and listening to every 12-inch single that came out in Italy, one by one, year by year—a time-consuming endeavour. So I thought, "Let me see what AI comes up with here; perhaps it can streamline this process."

What came back were indeed italo disco songs from the time period that I requested, some of which I hadn't heard before. Crucially, the songs were all corny. They were presented purely as raw data and lacked curation. I didn't enjoy a single track that the AI offered. Therein lies the pivotal flaw in this age where corporations are frantically scrambling to sneak AI into everything we use without our consent: The machine lacks discernment.

Not unlike the artless ghouls who delight in potentially disrupting the livelihoods of every artist on the planet, these apps are tasteless.

My personal taste has been forged and refined through countless positive and negative experiences that can't be replicated by an AI. My thought process around what I listen to is never linear or completely logical. What might profile as something that I usually appreciate could end up being too on-the-nose for me to actually enjoy. Conversely, I might be attracted to a song that outwardly appears to be at odds with everything I stand for. As much as streaming companies like Spotify see us as predictable lumps of flesh to be marketed to, no machine can truly anticipate the idiosyncrasies of the human mind.

A January 2023 edition of Nick Cave's newsletter *The Red Hand Files* found him responding to a fan who had asked ChatGPT to create a song in the style of Cave's music. His reply highlighted the inherently derivative nature of these apps, their technology totally reliant on scraping data from previously existing art: "ChatGPT's melancholy role is that it is destined to imitate and can never have an authentic human experience, no matter how devalued and inconsequential the human experience may in time become."

Doubtlessly, there will be a procession of keyboard cowboys eagerly replicating my prompt, desperately hoping to disprove my findings. Thankfully, they probably can't tell the difference between a good and bad song either. What they also don't seem to appreciate is that when it comes to art and life, the journey is just as important as the destination. As the *Globe*'s experiment proved, you can attempt to make a reasonable facsimile of my past work, but I'm an ever-changing artist, constantly evolving, forever influenced by my surroundings, experiences, and interests. New year, new me. No one could possibly predict my career trajectory because even I don't know where I will go from here. This mutability is precisely what defines the maverick artists of our time.

▸

Where I do sense a true existential threat from AI for musicians is in the world of the silver screen. Getting your song in a film, TV show, or commercial can be life-changing for an artist. My song "My Crew (Woooo)" was featured in both HBO's *Ballers* and *A Man Called Otto* starring Tom Hanks. These opportunities brought me significant mainstream exposure and a couple of the largest individual payments I've received in my life. In a music industry where our every income stream has been intentionally depleted by tech companies and corporations, "syncs" are among the last places where the pay is still sizeable for musicians.

That's one of the main reasons that this sector is so susceptible to AI. For a music supervisor, getting that perfect song into your film usually requires stacks of paperwork as well as negotiations between yourself and labels, publishers, artists, and rights owners. Dealing with all those humans often prolongs the process. With the development of generative apps like Suno, that friction is removed. You just give it a prompt, and the app creates a tailored backdrop for your scene at a fraction of the cost.

In advertising, musicians are already given briefs that ask them to create a sound-alike version of a given track for use in a commercial. Now, the ad companies can do the same thing without even hiring a musician. And you know that terrible interstitial music you hear on reality shows like *Selling Sunset* that already sounds AI-generated? I'm sure it will go completely A-pop in the not-so-distant future. What happens when the technology advances to the point that a director could upload a script and footage, and get an AI score created that properly soundtracks the action?

I'm sure AI would still fail to generate anything nearly as rich as award-winning composer Ludwig Göransson's Oscar-nominated score for director Ryan Coogler's thought-provoking, genre-hopping masterpiece *Sinners*.

With the film largely framed around the exploitation of Black musicians, Göransson crafted a score that functions as a transatlantic survey of modern music from Irish folk to gospel to hip-hop. It's informed as much by his childhood metal fandom as it is by a love of the blues shared by Göransson's father and Coogler's uncle. In an interview with the *Los Angeles Times*, Coogler gushed about the personal touches present in Göransson's score: "I love this score because I think it's infused with his love for music, his love for his dad, his love for his wife, his love for his kids. I can literally feel it in the music."

▶

Suno's website features the tagline "Suno is building a future where anyone can make great music," a wonderful example of the tech world's predilection for selling us something that we already have. I first learned about the app in a 2024 *Rolling Stone* piece that was borderline advertorial. In it, the company shared an example of its tech in which the prompt "solo acoustic Mississippi Delta blues about a sad AI" was used to generate a surprisingly authentic facsimile of a weathered Black voice wailing sorrowfully about being "a soul trapped in this circuitry."

The robotic blues singer's lyric appears to be a rather accurate description of the process that Suno uses to generate its AI songs. In a June 24, 2024, court filing in a lawsuit brought by Sony Music Group, Warner Music Group, and Universal Music Group, Suno admitted that its model was trained on copyrighted data from "tens of millions of recordings," all done without compensating the artists or labels. (Suno has since settled with WMG, leading to a partnership.) The app's "training data includes essentially all music files of reasonable quality that are accessible on the open Internet," meaning the platform wouldn't exist without the labour of countless flesh-and-blood musicians.

Suno argues that its industrial-scale data scraping constitutes fair use because the data is used in "creating an ultimately non-infringing new product." In a blog published in response to the court case, Suno was adamant about its dedication to fresh content, proudly citing "originality-guarding features" such as "checking for and preventing copyrighted content in audio uploads" as well as "disallowing artist-based descriptions in requests to generate music." It describes its app as helping users to "create music through a similar process to one humans have used forever: by learning styles, patterns, and forms (in essence, the 'grammar' of music), and then inventing new music around them."

In the court filing, Suno alleges that "no one owns musical styles." This brings to mind the infamous 2015 Pharrell Williams v. Bridgeport Music lawsuit where Marvin Gaye's family successfully argued that Robin Thicke and producer Pharrell Williams had copied the "feel" of Gaye's "Got To Give It Up" for their song "Blurred Lines." This ruling presented a dangerous new legal precedent, as copyright infringement in music had previously been restricted to the plagiarism of lyrics and melodies, not the vague and indefinable concept of two songs having a similar vibe. Gaye's family received $7.3 million in damages. In a world where the act of borrowing from existing songs has become newly vulnerable to legal action, Suno's growth as a music-industry disruptor resides on shaky ground.

The company loves to talk up its app's potential, promising "an explosion of new artists that are creating music in new ways, building fan bases, finding new reasons to smile, and getting famous." But after listening to the actual output from users of the app, I haven't encountered a song that could withstand any level of critical assessment. A recurring element in AI-generated songs is poor lyrics, curiously devoid of any shred of human character.

While Italo disco songs can be charming in their passionate attempts at the English language, Suno AI's clumsy verbiage feels clinical and uncanny. The technology appears to be capable of making only superficial observations. One Suno song I came across went "Yo, they still rockin' them dad jeans / Them high waters, I mean / Like, what the heck? / Bruh, embarrassing to the max." Suno struggles with metaphor and slang. The songs are united in their lack of compelling insight, sounding like generic radio fare but significantly more forgettable.

It's true that many italo disco songs are themselves derivative of previous hits. There are message board threads where listeners have posted dozens of songs that borrow more than just inspiration from massive '80s bangers. These pseudo-cover songs, with their pilfered melodies and similar lyrics, often actually share only passing resemblance to the originals. The artists use the hits as a jumping-off point for their strange diversions, making the italo disco versions another example of music as an oral tradition that is forever passed from culture to culture. Music is a conversation, and the italo disco songs are lovingly lost in translation.

The users of Suno that I've encountered online seem to have a lack of understanding of music conventions that makes it unlikely that they will generate anything worthwhile. An X user shared a Suno clip that was described as "Drum & Bass but at a 120 bpm pop tempo, so more like breakbeat," but it didn't sound like any of that stuff. It was a toothless knock-off of Evanescence and didn't actually have a drum break in it at all. Huh? A frustrated poster on the r/SunoAI subreddit complained that the app wasn't generating good results for his song with "12 verses of lyrics." Not being able to actually hear the song that he was griping about, I can't imagine what genre of music he could be attempting to create here. Another Redditor went viral for complaining about having to think up his own Suno prompts, which would remove the last remaining element of human intervention involved in using the AI.

Suno has effectively dropped the barrier of entry to create a composition, leading to a proliferation of low-quality AI-generated songs taking over YouTube, due to their monetization potential. An almost- twelve-hour-long video of inoffensive lo-fi beats from user the Japanese Town has nearly twenty million views, and none of the commenters appear to care about the origin of the music they're listening to. This user has over six hundred similar videos, each with an AI-generated image of a vaguely Tokyo-esque purple skyline with telltale mangled word salad text on the city's neon signs.

With Suno version 4.5, users can make surprisingly professional-sounding pop music; if you aren't listening closely, it loosely resembles an authentic radio single. But the AI songs are always missing what made smashes like Sabrina Carpenter's "Espresso" a hit: Carpenter and her co-writers' intentionally strange use of language. The song's chorus disjointedly compares the singer to the titular caffeinated beverage, there's an unconventional Mountain Dew pun, and she redefines the concept of not giving a fuck—quirks like these are smoothed out by AI to sound more like what the machine thinks a pop song is supposed to sound like. But these risks, such as the decision to keep a lyric about Sabrina working late because of her job as a singer, despite how seemingly random this declaration is, are what give real pop hits their animating energy.

In the aforementioned *Rolling Stone* piece, the journalist is careful to describe Suno's employees as being musically inclined: "Many Suno employees are musicians; there's a piano and guitars on hand in the office, and framed images of classical composers on the walls." I can't help but laugh when I picture staffers at a tech company that specializes in AI music walking past a portrait of Beethoven's piercing gaze all day, as if the interior decorating could ever possibly absolve them for what their company exists to do. It's reminiscent of former Spotify CEO Daniel Ek wearing a t-shirt with a drawing of a guitar on it during a 2015 Spotify event in New York. Tech moguls treat our tools as totems, protective talismans to justify their exploitation.

In a 2025 podcast interview with *20VC*, Suno CEO and co-founder Mikey Shulman shared his facile assessment of the music creation process: "It's not really enjoyable to make music now. It takes a lot of time, it takes a lot of practice, you need to get really good at an instrument or really good at a piece of production software. I think the majority of people don't enjoy the majority of time they spend making music." If I prompted ChatGPT to tell me, "What would an alien from a faraway planet say if I asked them to describe making music?," it might spit out something close to what Shulman said in the interview. The person who leads Suno is clearly flummoxed by the intangible magic of songwriting and can't even contemplate the joy one might feel from learning a skill over time. Making music is essentially problem-solving, a group of people searching for feeling out of the ether, who use their accumulated expertise to create something greater than themselves.

Those eureka moments when I've broken through a roadblock as I worked on a song have been some of the most exhilarating moments of my life. Executives like Shulman are ignorant to this feeling, blithely selling the world on their shaky understanding of what it means to be an artist. The creative process is one of the final frontiers left unconquered by an avaricious tech sector that seems desperate to monetize every corner of our lives. There will come a day when AI music becomes virtually indistinguishable from songs made by real people, but the intangible spark that can come only from the friction of human experience will still be noticeably absent.

▶

In April 2025, OpenAI introduced GPT-4o, a powerful image generator. Users learned that by prompting the AI to make art in the style of the famed Japanese animation company Studio Ghibli, they would be presented with high-quality images that were surprisingly close in style to filmmaker Hayao Miyazaki's work, leading to a surge of viral memes. Couples I knew ran their selfies through the AI to transform themselves into charming cartoons in the blink of an eye.

This was all done without Miyazaki's consent, allegedly by training the AI to scrape data from his films. This created a moral quagmire for some users while the more tech-inclined naturally saw it as an indicator of the likely death of the animation world. Miyazaki had addressed his thoughts on AI in 2016; that clip went viral in the wake of GPT-4o.

In the video, he's at a conference table watching a demonstration of a crude AI monster crawling across a screen, presented to him by the group of young animators who made it. His response was a withering rejoinder: "Whoever creates this stuff has no idea what pain is whatsoever. I am utterly disgusted . . . I would never wish to incorporate this technology into my work at all. I strongly feel that this is an insult to life itself."

In the documentary *10 Years with Hayao Miyazaki*, it's revealed that it took Studio Ghibli fifteen months to complete a four-second-long crowd scene. When Miyazaki works on a film, he brings decades of life experience with him that inform every scratch of his pencil. A Twitter thread with screenshots from the documentary shows countless examples of him struggling to work. But at one point while he's sketching, he says, "If life's hassles disappeared, you'd want them back."

For my wife's birthday in 2020, I commissioned a drawing from a visual artist named Ohara Hale, whom I befriended when I was living in Montréal. I asked Ohara to draw us in my partner's apartment with her cat Paddington Bear and suggested some activities and interests that could be referenced. Ohara totally smashed the brief. She drew us all in scrappy cartoon form, even including a doodle of me rapping to my partner. I took the image to a local print shop and got it framed at a gallery that has been in business for over three decades.

The stunned jubilance in my wife's eyes when I surprised her with that gift is something that I'll never forget. It proudly hangs in our family home today and stands as a reminder of how far we've come together, a priceless marker of time. The drawing is evocative, taking me back to that particular point in our lives whenever I see it. Unlike those GPT-4o memes that were everywhere in March but have faded away from my feed in the months since, I paid Ohara and had to wait a few weeks for the print to be produced. A bespoke piece of art handcrafted by human beings such as this might become a cherished rarity if the tech companies have their way.

It's true that artificial intelligence is evolving rapidly. At the time of writing, Google's Veo 3 video-generation model has launched to great fanfare with new audio capabilities, all shown off in a shocking demo clip that looks exactly like a regular TV commercial with human actors speaking dialogue. That is, if you don't focus on the mangled text on a banner in the background or the occasional dead-eyed demonic stare from one of the characters. Google's Gemini 3 Pro Image, also known as Nano Banana Pro, has shockingly robust image-editing capabilities. You can merge several images based on prompts, a technological advancement that could make Photoshop obsolete and have nefarious potential applications in the wrong hands. When you pit an example from the first version of Midjourney against what's available today, it's stunning just how primitive the original model looks in comparison with what developed in only three years.

Google DeepMind researcher Aleksander Holynski posted on X that he could use Google's Genie 3 software to go inside Edward Hopper's *Nighthawks*, making one of the most iconic pieces of American art look like a cheap first-person shooter game. This added nothing of value to the haunting, evocative original painting. One of the most gratifying parts of visiting an art museum is using your mind to imagine what lies beyond the frame: the intention behind the work, the context it sprang from, the experiences that led to its creation. Using AI tools in the way Holynski did shows the contempt that some have begun to have for their own imaginations.

It's possible that by the time you read this, AI has become less of a hot topic. Remember the hype around NFTs just a few years ago? It seemed like everywhere I turned, there was yet another startup looking to revolutionize life for musicians with an assist from the blockchain. There seems to be more public understanding about how AI works than there was around NFTs, which are still an abstract concept to the uninitiated. Plus the investment in AI is certainly much greater than the various Bored Ape scams and chicanery surrounding the NFT boom.

I suppose that's partly why corporations are cramming artificial intelligence into everything. On one hand, it's to make users more reliant on the tech so it becomes more difficult for us to divest. On the other, it's to justify the prior investment by these companies in the technology. Startups are more likely to get funding if their tech incorporates AI in some way. According to Silicon Valley Bank's "Innovation Economy Outlook Q1 2025" report, 48 percent of venture-capital funding went to AI-related companies in 2024. OpenAI, the team behind ChatGPT, received the largest private startup funding round in history with a $40 billion investment from SoftBank, announced in April 2025.

With AI becoming the financial engine for the tech sector, this unfettered growth has been at the expense of the natural world. AI training, use, and development exact a heavy environmental toll. According to a 2025 *MIT News* report, the servers at data centres are estimated to consume 1,050 terawatts annually in 2026, putting their energy usage at fifth place on the global list between Japan and Russia. All that electricity means more carbon dioxide in the atmosphere.

And these servers require massive amounts of water to cool them down. In a 2025 paper called "Making AI Less 'Thirsty': Uncovering and Addressing the Secret Water Footprint of AI Models," it's stated that "water withdrawal of global AI is projected to reach 4.2–6.6 billion cubic meters in 2027, which is more than the total annual water withdrawal of four to six Denmarks or half of the U.K."

The environmental impact has already hit the communities where these data centres are placed. Elon Musk's xAI company has built a supercomputer near the predominantly Black neighbourhood known as Boxtown in Memphis to train its Grok AI chatbot. According to *Futurism*, this includes "35 portable gas-powered turbines with enough electricity output between them to power a small city, spewing harmful, smog-forming pollutants into the air, including nitrogen oxides and formaldehyde." One resident remarked, "I can't breathe at home, it smells like gas outside."

Beyond what AI is doing to our bodies, it is also having an effect on our cognition. I've noticed users on X asking Grok for the context of a post more often, rather than doing their own research. Two commenters asked Grok the same question and received contradictory answers. In these highly polarized times, folks are turning to Grok to give them information uncoloured by the bias that taints nearly every person-to-person interaction on the platform. That might have been somewhat plausible before Elon Musk gave Grok a system update that caused it to post antisemitic comments and refer to itself as "MechaHitler." Relying on any form of man-made tech to tell us right from wrong is a risky proposition.

In an essay published in *New Socialist* entitled "AI: The New Aesthetics of Fascism," author Gareth Watkins examines the right wing's predilection for AI slop, the low-quality, spammy, artificially generated content that is filling up every social media platform like a poop-choked septic tank: "The right wing aesthetic project is to flood the zone . . . in order to erode the intellectual foundations for resisting political cruelty."

Case in point: The Trump White House's official X account and its newfound love of shitposting. Alongside a strangely informal comedic tone, it turned to the Miyazaki AI filter to depict an ICE officer deporting a real-life woman in cartoon form.

Another post features an AI-generated photo of a row of alligators wearing ICE ball caps in front of a prison in a nod to "Alligator Alcatraz," a controversial ICE detention centre located in the Florida Everglades. The ease of generating AI images has made it possible for the most heartless people in the world to weaponize art, facilitating heretofore unseen levels of distasteful cruelty. If Hitler were alive today, he might be churning out AI slop instead of shitty paintings.

Artificial intelligence has also shaken the foundations of higher education. ChatGPT has become a go-to resource for students worldwide, as described in detail in *New York Magazine*'s article "Everyone Is Cheating Their Way Through College." A student quoted in that piece justified using AI to help with a university assignment by comparing it to building a house with power tools.

AI may be on the verge of rendering homework obsolete, but it remains to be seen what we lose from not struggling through the process without performance-enhancing tech. An SBS Swiss Business School study called "AI Tools in Society: Impacts on Cognitive Offloading and the Future of Critical Thinking" suggests that "individuals who depend too heavily on AI to perform analytical tasks may become less proficient at engaging in deep, independent analysis. This reliance can lead to a superficial understanding of information and reduce the capacity for critical analysis."

An MIT study called "Your Brain on ChatGPT: Accumulation of Cognitive Debt when Using an AI Assistant for Essay Writing Task" tested the brain activity of three groups focused on their SAT essay writing. One group used ChatGPT, another used Google search, and the last group used neither in their essays. The group that only used their brains to write "reported higher satisfaction and demonstrated higher brain connectivity, compared to other groups," while the essays written by the ChatGPT users "carried a lesser significance or value to the participants" who later struggled to correctly quote their own essays.

I certainly could've asked ChatGPT to write this essay for me. But if I did that, I would have missed out on the joys of doing research. I wouldn't have had all those laughs I got from listening to AI music! ChatGPT wouldn't have known or included that story about the birthday drawing I had commissioned for my wife. When companies started rolling out self-service checkout kiosks so they could cut down on employees, they would often stick a worker there to monitor customer behaviour and to make sure the machines were operating correctly.

That has become our role whenever we prompt an AI to do something for us. We're helping it learn how to do our jobs for us, the older model overseeing our replacements. In a *Gizmodo* piece about how artificial intelligence is impacting work, self-described "AI automation marketing advisor" Elijah Clark delighted at the worker-displacing potential of the new technology: "AI doesn't go on strike. It doesn't ask for a pay raise."

Tech companies are marketing AI as a wonderful new innovation. "Work happy with Zoom AI Companion" says an ad I see in the app during a meeting. Will I be happier with the AI taking notes of everything we said than I would be if I took them myself? What happens when I look back and points were misinterpreted by the technology, as has happened to friends of mine? This idea that we should be delighted by machines making life more convenient leaves out the fact that this friction is actually the juice that life is made of.

Whenever I'm downtown in Toronto, I see legions of fast-food couriers zipping around with orders at all hours of the day. I understand that work and life circumstances can make it helpful to order things from time to time, but what happens when you go and pick up your food yourself?

You might come across a beautiful flower emerging in springtime. Maybe you bump into a friend and make plans for a get-together. I often get ideas when I walk, the forward motion shaking loose the cobwebs. When you arrive at the restaurant, you could have a thought-provoking conversation with the restaurateur and build a friendship with them. There's an ocean of possibilities. The journey isn't just about getting from point A to point B.

The Suno CEO's words about how making music isn't enjoyable have continued to echo in my mind. It's true that there are times when you curse the day that you decided to become a musician. Your gear doesn't cooperate, the ideas aren't flowing, and you feel like the whole thing is a fool's errand. But anyone who loves the craft accepts those low moments in exchange for the incredible highs that come with making something that is truly transcendent or pushing yourself to do something you didn't think you were capable of.

My attempts at optimizing my music discovery practice using AI were fruitless. Even as the technology improves over time, I can't see myself going that route. Without using AI, I could spend an entire day searching for songs, only come away with one or two, and not see it as a waste of time. Maybe I saw some inspiring album art along the way that might influence the aesthetic for my next release. I might discover some '80s outsider musician and then find out that he's performing in my city later this month after not playing live for forty years.

The nonlinear nature of the hunt is what makes it endlessly entertaining. And the songs that do end up being useful for me are imbued with much more meaning than they would be if I sourced them any other way. I believe that my enthusiasm is transferred to them when I play them for others. The excitement is contagious. Maybe in five or ten years, people will use the chip in their brain to skim through this essay and see it as anachronistic. But I believe that we don't get enough life to let the machines live it for us.

Listening to Music with a Calculator

DJ Akademiks is not a journalist, and crucially, he isn't known for his DJing. Born Livingston Allen in Spanish Town, Jamaica, the nerdy rap fan based in New Jersey developed a substantial online following of young men through his podcasting and social media accounts over the past decade. Starting out as a college radio jock who would throw parties as a student at Rutgers University in 2013, he was kicked off the air for his fiery commentary as well as for playing ribald songs like Big Sean's "Dance (A$$)" that ran afoul of FCC standards. He stokes controversy with his takes on YouTube—his 2014 video series "The War in Chiraq" was criticized for enflaming gang conflict in Chicago.

Akademiks found a wider audience as one of the hosts of Complex's *Everyday Struggle* in 2017, where he espoused an outsider perspective in contrast to the more commercial-leaning Joe Budden. Since leaving that show, Akademiks has become a leading figure in hip-hop culture who discusses the news of the day from his gaming chair during his livestreams while occasionally chugging a bottle of Hennessy in a blustery performance that falls somewhere between the theatrical ranting of sports pundits like Stephen A. Smith and the conspiratorial ramblings of right-wing politicos such as Alex Jones.

Allen could be seen as the first hip-hop shock jock, having more in common with Howard Stern than he does with Funkmaster Flex. He runs a social media empire that includes his X and Instagram pages as well as those of AkademiksTV, the "Official News/Updates Channel for the Akademy," which functions as a kind of propaganda wing allegedly run by a fan known as @grandwizardchatnigga. A clip from Akademiks's Twitch stream was featured on "Control" from Playboi Carti's highly anticipated 2020 album *Whole Lotta Red*, cementing Ak as one of hip-hop's most recognizable voices.

In recent years, Akademiks has tilted in a more conservative direction. Like Andrew Tate before him, he has moved from Twitch to Rumble to avoid the former's strict content guidelines. He has posted videos of Trump to his pages. Ak infamously met with Ye for a March 2025 interview where West answered the door while wearing an iced-out swastika chain around his neck. Ak didn't blink when Ye went into another room and returned in full black KKK regalia.

Increased exposure to the Akademiks brand uncovers his apparent tendency towards misogyny, particularly in commentary about artists like Megan Thee Stallion that wouldn't look out of place on an incel message board. In 2024, Allen was accused of sexual assault and defamation in an ongoing civil suit. In a Rumble livestream responding to the lawsuit, he denied any wrongdoing, called it "a shakedown" and claimed that he was an "innocent man." He was met with grooming allegations for inappropriate sexual comments he made to a 15-year-old boy during one of his livestreams the following year, leading to an apology where he called it a "teachable moment" and a "very regretful moment."

Akademiks makes hip-hop news entertainment in the tradition of *TMZ*, profiting from gossip, conflict, and death. Not following him can make you feel out of touch with what's happening in the culture, but letting him into your feed means you're exposed to the most toxic corners of hip-hop and the retrograde attitudes of his audience in the comments. And his successful approach has been copied by legions of hip-hop platforms. Streamers and YouTubers like Akademiks are the new tastemakers of rap. Independent, down-to-earth, and accessible, they are seen by their audience as an antidote to the staid gatekeepers of traditional music media. But unlike legitimate music journalists, they often only have opinions to offer.

▶

The legendary late music critic Greg Tate didn't deal in hot takes. Often referred to as the godfather of hip-hop journalism, his freewheeling style and unquestioned authority were forged through his experiences studying journalism at Howard University, on the ground as a member of New York City's music scene in the '80s, and during his time writing album reviews for the *Village Voice*.

Tate had a long, decorated career contributing to publications like *Rolling Stone*, *VIBE*, the *New York Times*, the *Washington Post*, and *Artforum*. In the process, he helped to elevate hip-hop from the "fad" that it was initially perceived to be into a movement worthy of seriousness by expertly connecting it to the lineage of the Black genres that preceded it. His reputation as a critic was hard-earned over many years, and he built it by imbuing anything he wrote about with a higher level of significance. Flea from Red Hot Chili Peppers broke into tears upon learning that *Californication* had been reviewed in *Rolling Stone* by the esteemed Tate.

Comparatively, streamers lack expertise. Shackled to a visual medium, their success is largely based on their utility as entertainers and personalities, not on their knowledge. They can be amusing, but they are rarely insightful. Some dance and mug in front of their webcams, while others grab attention through gimmicks. But they are united in their reverence for the present; history is of little use to a livestreamer who gets paid by his viewers in the chat in real time. No subject can keep their attention long enough to be deeply considered. On to the next one.

Monetization by video-streaming platforms has ironically meant a galaxy of creators give similar takes about the same albums and the same news, a heliocentric new media model that still benefits the biggest stars with the strongest gravitational pull. Whatever gets the most eyeballs wins. That's why you find massive celebrities like Kim Kardashian, who built her fanbase primarily through reality TV, showing up to hang out on Twitch at Kai Cenat's "streaming mansion" in front of his 20.2 million followers instead of going on *The Late Show with Stephen Colbert*, the highest-rated late night TV program, which averaged 2.42 million viewers in the second quarter of 2025. Looking at Cenat's Twitch stream, you can see how many hundreds of thousands of people are watching in real time, the number fluctuating like a stock ticker.

All you need today is a laptop, a camera, a microphone, and an internet connection, and you too can monetize your takes. The viewer's trust is earned through the size of a streamer's audience or repeated exposure to a streamer's platform, not through their knowledge or experience. And as legacy publications continue to fold, the audience for streamers like Akademiks has only grown.

Much of it comes down to numbers—and not just viewership stats. In many of his posts, Akademiks has been a major proponent of sales equalling quality. An example can be found in this Instagram caption sharing a screencap from Chart Data's X page:

Lil Baby sells 140k first week.
Bad Bunny sells 122k first week

Akademiks often uses first week sales numbers to shift perceptions and imply connections that may or may not be there. That particular Lil Baby album, *WHAM*, wasn't warmly received by critics. This Ak post showing that he actually outsold superstar Bad Bunny could be seen as an attempt to burnish the rapper's reputation after a less-than-stellar release.

Allen's cozy relationship with Drake in particular demonstrates his implicit lack of impartiality. In a December 1, 2024, post to his AkademiksTV X account, a graphic was shared featuring Drake's *For All the Dogs* album cover with "412k" next to a picture of Drizzy smiling while staring at his phone with the following caption:

KENDRICK LAMAR SELLS 319K FIRST WEEK
CEMENTING THE WEST COAST FLOP.

Kendrick, Dj mustard, YG, schoolboy q, ab soul and doechi
all fail to outsell Drake combined.

Selling 179,000 more first week units than Lil Baby is considered a failure when it's done by one of Drake's adversaries. AkademiksTV is weaponizing sales data to suggest Kendrick Lamar's *GNX* was a flop in an intentionally misleading way, not unlike how Fox News might use a false equivalency to get one of their talking points across. Predictably, this pissed off Kendrick's fans and got them to comment, enriching Akademiks in the process. At press time, the post has 1.1 million impressions.

User @syllawebster quote-tweeted that post with the perfect response:

"Stop listening to music with a calculator."

▶

Take a moment to consider your thought process when you choose something to listen to. It's likely changed in recent years, due to streaming app design that deprioritizes the search function and guides us toward AI playlists and away from our own curation. But barring that, what does it usually take to get you to press Play?

Probably the most influential determining factor for me is word of mouth. I have a coterie of music nerds in my social circle who have rarely steered me wrong, and I unreservedly trust their opinions when they enthusiastically praise something. I never ignore a personal recommendation. It turns out that this attitude is actually quite common. In Nielsen's "2021 Trust in Advertising Study," 88 percent of respondents were most likely to trust recommendations that came from people that they know.

In an age when the human touch is being phased out and replaced by AI playlist curators, you've gotta take the IRL picks wherever you can get them. Celebrity endorsements can also be effective. If Frank Ocean posts a photo of a song playing on his car stereo to his Instagram story, I will practically race to my favourite app to hear what he's into. And music criticism is still hanging in there, though the influence of the biggest publications seems to be waning in recent years as listeners and journalists have become increasingly ensconced in their own silos.

One thing I've never thought was, "Hmm, this album sold a lot of records. Maybe I should check it out." Historically, it's been rare to see the best-selling records among the most well reviewed. The top-selling acts of the '90s were Mariah Carey, Céline Dion, and Garth Brooks, all popular artists who weren't the critical darlings of their time. Michael Jackson's *Thriller* is probably the biggest outlier; you could also look to the Beatles' discography for a direct correlation between high quality of art and large quantity sold.

But after a few hours of wading through today's increasingly toxic online discourse, you might come away with the idea that sales numbers are by far the most important marker of quality for music fans. The discourse around new album releases has devolved into a morass of faceless avatars spouting industry jargon at each other online, civilians cosplaying as major label execs and A&Rs when they actually have no professional stake in the chart performance of whatever pop single they're evangelizing for.

There are fan pages like ThuggerDaily, a one-person fan club run by an anonymous twenty-five-year-old Texan known as Bliv, whose thoughtful coverage of Young Thug's RICO trial as an amateur legal reporter on Twitter earned him a profile in *The New Yorker* that compared him to Joseph Pulitzer. His page's success has led to copycat accounts focused on other Atlanta rappers Lil Baby and Gunna.

The Art of Dialogue posts interview clips featuring musicians and celebrities that they produce as well as those from other sources. Their captions stand out for their use of unusually pointed language that you wouldn't see at a traditional news outlet:

> Aries Spears, who hasn't been relevant since MadTV in the '90s,
> goes on an emotional rant after Ice Cube calls him a 'sucka'
> for saying he didn't like him as a rapper or actor.

I found over twenty posts about Spears sent from the Art of Dialogue to its nearly 200,000 X followers, including one that erroneously referred to the comedian as being "openly gay." This possibly stems from a May 2025 DJ Vlad interview where Spears dissed the Art of Dialogue for its habit of clipping videos and sharing them outside their original context. Unlike legacy news outlets that have rigorous editorial standards, hip-hop blogs and social media pages are not opposed to publicly leaning into their biases. If you run afoul of someone who controls one of these pages, there are no checks and balances to prevent them from targeting you.

On Instagram, the Art of Dialogue's bio sports an email that you can contact "for business." This is a common sight on pages like these, and the implication is that you can pay to have your artist or yourself featured. After being pressed by pgLang co-founder and Kendrick Lamar collaborator Dave Free at a Grand National Tour show in Detroit about whether or not he was on Drake's payroll, DJ Akademiks denied it on his livestream, saying, "We don't do pay-for-play. You can't buy my opinion. I've always said, 'The moment you could buy my opinion, I don't matter.'"

Yet whenever I see an unknown artist nabbing coveted space on the Akademiks Instagram page promoted to his 5.2 million followers, I comb the comments for the inevitable: "He paid for this post 😂😂😂."

Conversely, Aries Spears told Vlad during their interview that one of the reasons he prefers going on his channel is because Vlad pays him. Baton Rouge rapper Boosie Badazz claimed that he "could make half a million with Vlad every year" if he wanted to. Vlad has said he would pay $100,000 to secure the first interview with Diddy when he gets out of prison. During a livestream, Boosie claimed that he currently charges $45,000 to be interviewed on a podcast.

To a certain extent, this is understandable in the contemporary digital landscape where a viral clip of you posted by someone else could make them rich and leave you with nothing. But professional journalists don't pay for interviews, referring to the practice as "chequebook journalism"; such a transaction could compromise the integrity of their reporting. It has typically been the domain of tabloid newspapers, but nowadays, the concept has gone digital.

Social media accounts and personalities like Chart Data, Talk of the Charts, Pop Base, Pop Crave, Kurrco, and DJ Akademiks are mostly content aggregators, resharing what artists post on social media as their own content. But one major and consistent part of the content strategy for these accounts is the way that they repurpose sales data, intentionally enflaming and emboldening various fandoms across the stanosphere into commenting, liking, and sharing their posts. It's a prime example of how, on today's internet, cruelty is rewarded.

These pages market themselves as sources for daily music news and updates, but what this form of online discourse actually does is cultivate a hostile social media environment where first week sales have been turned into something that the audience cares about and posts about, where the winners are those who sell the most records and the losers are only mentioned to highlight their futility.

In September 2024, Tommy Richman, coming off the success of two hit singles, released his debut album. He opted to take a risk by leaving his singles off, attempting to let his artistry speak for itself. It backfired mightily, all but muffling the buzz that he had previously garnered. And the blogs were first in line to publicly humiliate him for it. Kurrco posted "Tommy Richman's debut album 'COYOTE' reportedly sold ~3.4K units first week 📈" seemingly with the expectation that the internet would pile on and clown the "Million Dollar Baby" singer. At the time of writing, that post had 1.1 million impressions on X. That platform monetizes and incentivizes outrage through its Creator Revenue Sharing program, an Elon Musk innovation that allows users who pay for premium blue check accounts to profit from their posts.

I'd predict that many of the people who saw Kurrco's post were unaware that Tommy Richman had even released his album. I know I was. This post likely succeeded in tainting the public's perception of the release before they'd even heard it, while subsequently influencing how it will be listened to in the future.

Not all albums are hits right away. Now considered an all-time classic of East Coast hip-hop, Nas's *Illmatic* sold a paltry 59,000 units in its first week in 1994. Its longevity was secured by universal critical praise and underground street buzz. Most of my favourite albums didn't resonate with me on first listen; it was only after some time and repeated exposure that things clicked into place.

Lorde's *Melodrama*, a dense, writerly art pop album, didn't connect with me upon its initial 2017 release but has since burrowed its way past my defences almost a decade later. Would I have even bothered to put myself through the trouble of listening again if an account I trusted made a post implying how crappy it was right after it came out?

▶

To consider how we arrived at the point where sales are seen as a definitive measure of quality, we have to examine the past. Started in 1958, the *Billboard* Hot 100 chart evolved from several early incarnations to become the first reliable way to evaluate the success of music singles through retail sales and radio play. Sire Records founder and journalist Seymour Stein, discussing his part in creating the chart in an interview with Billboard.com, said the Hot 100 was originally designed as a tool for music industry insiders to quickly assess purchasing trends and to see which singles were most popular. In his words, the *Billboard* Hot 100 was "a guide to potential, as well as the current hits."

Billboard would call all the megastores and the mom-and-pop record shops in America directly to ask for ranked lists of what they thought were the best-selling releases that week. As you can imagine, this process was vulnerable to corruption and manipulation. According to former *Billboard* editor-in-chief Timothy White in an interview with the *New York Times*, some record store employees were "bribed with clock radios and all sorts of amenities and favors" if they juiced the numbers.

On May 25, 1991, *Billboard* started to factor in Nielsen SoundScan (now known as Luminate), which provided point-of-sale retail data scanned at the register through barcodes, into its albums chart and eventually all its charts, including the Hot 100 singles chart. In a 1996 *New York Times* piece, SoundScan founder Michael Shalett described the difference in *Billboard* reporting practices before and after SoundScan as being like going from "campfire" to "nuclear power."

The new system wasn't exactly foolproof. Rumours of labels buying thousands of their own CDs and dumping them in a warehouse to guarantee a number one debut persisted. Tommy Boy Records founder Tom Silverman accused record labels of buying their own digital singles on iTunes to help them rise up the charts in a 2010 interview with *Wired*.

Malfeasance aside, SoundScan's arrival still revolutionized and professionalized the sales reporting process, generating accurate numbers for the charts for the first time in *Billboard*'s history and subsequently bringing a new significance to first week sales.

Just a year before SoundScan's debut, the industry was crowning the likes of Milli Vanilli, MC Hammer, Vanilla Ice, and New Kids on the Block. The introduction of SoundScan levelled the playing field, immediately leading to a more sonically diverse set of artists topping the charts. It better reflected the changing mores of the American music listenership in the early '90s, capturing favourites such as Nirvana, N.W.A., Metallica, Garth Brooks, and Ice Cube. It was a sea change. Labels used this new data to aid in their marketing efforts, and fans' interest in watching the charts turned them into an unintentional audience to what was an industry resource published in a music trade publication.

The formula for the chart was significantly altered when digital downloads were included in the tabulations in 2005. Two years later, *Billboard* incorporated streaming data for the first time. (As of January 2026, YouTube streams no longer factor into the *Billboard* charts.) When it compiles its weekly charts today, *Billboard* includes downloads and streams with physical sales data by using two metrics: Track Equivalent Albums (ten song downloads from an album count as one album sale) and Streaming Equivalent Albums (1,250 paid song streams or 3,750 free tier song streams are equal to one album sale).

All of those changes set the stage for what would become the watershed moment for fan awareness of first week sales: the 50 Cent–Kanye West (now known as Ye) chart battle of September 11, 2007.

There had been one-on-one competitions for the top spot on the charts in the past. Blur and Oasis famously tried to settle the Battle of Britpop by pitting their new singles against each other back in August 1995. ("Country House" by Blur came out on top.) But a sales faceoff had never been so central to the marketing of two albums as it was between Ye's *Graduation* and 50 Cent's *Curtis*.

The rappers were featured on the cover of *Rolling Stone* in a confrontational pose that mimicked a boxing promo. Similar to Oasis vs. Blur and their class dichotomy, the perceived ideological differences between the artists added stakes to the friendly competition. 50 represented the status quo of New York gangsta rap in the wake of his world-conquering *Get Rich or Die Tryin'* while Ye had been incrementally ushering in a more artful vision for conscious hip-hop following the paradigm shift of *The College Dropout*. The two poles of the culture went head-to-head, the corporate face from the birthplace of the genre versus the flashy outsider from Chicago, a city with a comparatively less defined hip-hop history at the time. The industry couldn't have dreamt up something better.

When Ye won with a commanding 957,000 to 50 Cent's 691,000 first week sales, it was as if the culture had chosen a direction for itself. Violence, drug dealing, and guns were suddenly out of style. A new wave of alternative rap pointed the way forward, all led by the left-field fashionista who hired Takashi Murakami to design his album cover.

The fans who helped Ye to victory by buying his album were now cemented as part of rap history, forever tied to a music moment with reverberations that can still be felt today.

Launched on September 14, 1998, MTV's *Total Request Live* is usually remembered as the place where the biggest stars of the early twenty-first century would come to perform and promote their hits. I can picture its iconic Times Square studio in my mind's eye: the nonthreateningly affable host Carson Daly carefully trying to maintain decorum in the midst of chaos, the hundreds of frenzied fans on the street below, the ecstatic vibrancy of the Y2K fashion. But the most novel aspect of *TRL* was its role in democratizing music through the video-requesting concept that was the show's premise.

Learning what the audience thinks about popular music has been a long-standing objective of the record industry. An early televised example of this was a segment on *American Bandstand* called "Rate a Record" where they'd bring up a fan from the crowd and ask them to score a new song on a scale of 35 to 98. But rather than programming the show using that week's *Billboard* chart data like they did on *American Bandstand*, MTV's *TRL* encouraged viewers to go online, call, or fax to request their favourite songs and then tune in the next day to see if their video made the cut.

The result was a shift toward bubblegum pop acts like Christina Aguilera, Backstreet Boys, Britney Spears, and *NSync, who all had passionate fan followings of primarily young girls. Just as the introduction of SoundScan had changed what America considered a chart-topping act, *TRL*'s request system redefined what an MTV star looked like. It became a way for label executives to check the temperature of the CD-buying audience on a daily basis. It also introduced fans to the idea that they held the power to materially impact the success of their favourite artists, paving the way for shows like *American Idol* and *The Voice*.

As television's influence on the music industry receded with the rise of the internet—YouTube launched in 2005, and *TRL* went off the air in 2008—fan participation became more pronounced in the chart battles that followed Ye and 50 Cent's legendary tilt. Spotify became the most popular streaming service in the 2010s, and along with it came a focus on public play counts, allowing fans to see how their favourite new singles are faring on a daily basis.

▶

Today's fans follow the chart placements of their favourite musicians like a trader watches the stock market. This parasocial engagement is part of a larger commodification and gamification of every corner of life. Listeners root for their favourite artists to top the charts with a competitive fervour that is matched only by sports fandom and political partisanship.

This rise in fan obsession over chart dominance coincides with a time when our political leadership and traditional authority figures have spectacularly failed young people in the Western world, struggling to capture the popular imagination. After Kamala Harris lost to Donald Trump despite gaining Taylor Swift's endorsement, the Swifties likely believe that streaming a single three thousand times a day or buying multiple copies of the same album is a more impactful action than voting once for a political candidate, a uniquely tiresome exercise where even when you win, you still lose.

As it stands right now, choosing a political representative requires you to make a decision between candidates who will ignore you while expecting your fealty, doing nothing to materially improve your life after you've begrudgingly helped to lift them to power, and those who will gleefully pull out all the stops on their first day in office to wantonly destroy absolutely everything that you hold near and dear. The voting process is intentionally made as difficult as possible, held primarily during a finite time frame on a single day during working hours. And that's without even factoring in voter-suppression tactics like gerrymandering.

The alternative is to luxuriate in the world of musicians, athletes, and other celebrities, those deified beings who represent an idealized human experience, both aspirational and inspiring, especially when compared to the drudgery of twenty-first-century existence. Supporting your favourite artist is something that you can control; you can do it from the comfort of your home with the click of a button. Unlike volunteering for a political party, joining up with your fellow Angels online to help run the numbers up on Charli's various *Brat* singles is immediately rewarding. The pop charts have gone from an insider concern to the ultimate distraction.

Sales numbers are cited in stan wars by fans as a definitive metric for the supremacy of their faves. After SZA posted about Mercury retrograde and unexpectedly set off a torrent of abuse from Nicki Minaj in what could be considered a proxy war in the Drake–Kendrick Lamar conflict, their fans fought alongside them. When SZA predictably got terrorized by the Barbs, her fans clapped back with detailed comparison charts of each artist's total ticket revenue from recent tours and streaming data. Stans rarely make subjective claims as to why their favourite artist is the greatest; they come armed with verified objective data (which can be wilfully misrepresented or cherry-picked in whichever way benefits their argument).

Nicki suggested that SZA was manipulating her streaming numbers with "botted enhancements." A similar accusation was lobbed by AkademiksTV when the page pointed out that Kendrick Lamar had over a billion fewer monthly Spotify streams in August 2025 when compared to February of the same year. (He had played the Super Bowl halftime show that month, explaining the temporary boost in streams.) During the bombshell leak of Young Thug's alleged prison phone calls,

Thug allegedly admitted to paying $50,000 for fake streams to help his artist Gunna's album *DS4EVER* debut at number one on the Billboard 200 over The Weeknd's *Dawn FM* because he "got the plug on that."

A 2020 NPR report shined a light on a chart manipulation tactic employed in South Korea known as sajaegi. The term describes the practice of illegally bulk-buying essential items and has become shorthand for when a K-pop act hires a company to falsely boost their sales for chart placement through the use of hacking or "stream farms"—rooms full of countless phones logged into different user accounts, each playing the same track to boost a song's streaming numbers. It's becoming more difficult to discern how many superfans are real people and not bots or record label PR engaging in an astroturfing campaign.

K-pop fans have used sajaegi-like tactics in their quest to help their favourite acts get to the top, such as streaming a song repeatedly. This fan behaviour has crossed over to North America and has even been promoted by artists themselves; Justin Bieber shared fan-made graphics that instructed his legion of listeners to create a playlist with his 2020 single "Yummy" and let it play overnight while they sleep.

Bieber also skirted the ethical boundary of what constitutes a record sale with his creative bundling offers; he sold signed CD singles paired with a digital download for three dollars apiece. "Yummy" debuted at number two on the *Billboard* Hot 100, blocked by Roddy Ricch's "The Box." Beating the pride of Stratford, Ontario, at his own game, Travis Scott's *JackBoys 2* edged Bieber's *Swag* for the number one spot on the *Billboard* 200 in July 2025 with the help of no less than twenty-three different versions of the mixtape, including variants with alternate covers and bundles that included shirts and hoodies. Scott has gamed the system so many times with this strategy that people on X have taken to calling him "Bundle Man."

Legendary music industry iconoclast Prince actually started the bundling madness in earnest back in 2004 when he gave away his album *Musicology* for free with every ticket sold to his tour, selling 633,000 units and peaking at the number three spot on the *Billboard* 200. This ticket method is no longer allowed. Since then, artists and their fans have gone to increasingly desperate ends to climb the charts, sometimes directly competing against other acts and their fandoms in the process.

Taylor Swift released six new variants of *The Tortured Poets Department* that were geo-locked to the U.K. and only available for twenty-four hours on the week's final day of sales tracking when it looked as if Charli xcx would top that country's charts with *Brat*; Swift blocked Charli from the top spot. Swift similarly made three new vinyl variants of The *Life of a Showgirl* available for a single day in a move that appeared to be an attempt at preventing Tate McRae's deluxe version of *So Close to What* from ousting Swift from her seven-week-long perch at number one. Sabrina Carpenter's fans mobilized to block Travis Scott's rerelease of *Days Before Rodeo* from debuting at number one so *Short and Sweet* would be crowned the best-selling release for that week.

▶

I was late to the party with Spotify. Its Canadian launch in 2014 landed right in the middle of my five-year hiatus from releasing music. By the time I had properly re-emerged and signed with Entertainment One in 2016, Spotify had become a central figure in the Canadian music industry. It was all anyone wanted to talk about. After putting out "My Crew (Woooo)" as my comeback single in 2017, I began using the app in earnest, hoping to gain a deeper understanding of how it worked ahead of the release of my self-titled album in 2018.

The play counts for each of my songs were all publicly visible, along with my monthly listener count—directly below my artist name and header photo. The monthly listener number was given prominent placement, as if it were my occupation on a resumé. Little did I know that the availability of these numbers would become the bane of my life as a musician.

As an organized, data-oriented person, I did get a kick out of Spotify for Artists, its back-end tool for musicians. I could look at graphs of how many plays and listeners I had over a given time period, and I could see for the first time what my most popular songs actually were, a previously opaque concept. I could learn what cities and countries were playing my music the most. Spotify seemed to be a powerful platform that could potentially distribute my music to thousands of new fans across the planet. "My Crew (Woooo)" was added to marquee playlists like Hip-Hop Central and had been streamed hundreds of thousands of times. I had no way to contact these listeners, but at least I knew that they existed.

I quickly realized that Spotify had the music industry in a chokehold. I was encouraged by an A&R to tag Canadian Spotify employees whenever I posted about one of my tracks on social media in the hopes that they might appreciate the shout-out and send more playlisting our way. Who knows if this ever actually worked? It was happening to one Spotify Canada higher-up so much that he made it impossible to tag him on Instagram.

Even if some folks over there didn't ask for it, there was a strange fealty that artists were expected to give to Spotify. The company held lavish Christmas parties with free food, drinks, and impressive live entertainment. Our careers were at the whim of the playlist curators. They reminded me of the Wizard of Oz, a mysterious, omnipotent being who held outsized power over my life.

The urge to compare stats with my peers was too great to resist. The existence of this tool seemed designed solely to make me feel inferior. If comparison is the thief of joy, this tool was the supercharged joy destroyer of my nightmares. I'd pit myself against old indie rock pals from Montréal, other rappers in Toronto, world-famous pop stars, and new artists I'd recently learned of. These Spotify design elements seemed as if they were created to inspire unhealthy competition.

The twenty-eight-day cycle encouraged me to release music more frequently to maintain a healthy number of monthly listeners. It felt like topping up a draining bathtub with a carafe of water. When the number was high, life was great. When it lagged, it felt like my relevance as a musician was evaporating on a daily basis. The number also impacted how I assessed other musicians who reached out to me—a high number indicating that they were a professional artist who was worth taking seriously.

My monthly listener count was scrutinized by festival curators, booking agents, managers, and show promoters who all stopped by my artist page to briskly gauge whether or not I was worth going into business with. It probably never crossed their minds that much of this listenership was derived from playlists and algorithmic recommendations, including folks who weren't intentionally listening to my music, making it an inexact methodology to determine the size of my audience.

This obsession with growth metrics, a hallmark of the ever-scalable world of tech, also extended to Instagram, TikTok, and X. The music world I had returned to after my hiatus had been forever changed. I used to occasionally adjudicate grant applicants, and I noticed that in the section about their career goals, the aspiring musicians were suddenly looking for followers and streams when the focus had been on fans and record sales only a few years prior. My early albums were critically acclaimed, and I had a reputation for being a strong live performer. But those basic tenets of being a career musician didn't hold as much weight in the streaming era.

When Pusha T and Malice reunited as Clipse to put out 2025's *Let God Sort Em Out*, their first album together in over fifteen years, the duo returned to a vastly changed music ecosystem. They came up during the time when you could just hop on MTV, maybe stop by BET's *Rap City: The Basement*, do a couple magazine interviews, and be done with it. They approached this new rollout with vigour: hitting the podcast circuit, doing brand collabs with Carhartt and Adidas, and connecting with all the legacy media outlets for interviews.

When the album finally dropped on July 11, 2025, to wide audience approval, the usual suspects were lining up online to decide whether or not it was a sales flop. One page posted that Clipse were "on pace to sell 90K" in the first week, pegging them at the fourth spot on the *Billboard* 200 charts, which a commenter said "def exceeded my projections." Clipse re-emerged into a world where regular people now made sales projections for albums.

Various accounts with divergent agendas argued about whether Clipse landing fourth after such an extensive rollout was a horrendous failure or a major W. One X user pointed out the hypocrisy of the people who roundly mocked Lil Wayne's poorly received *Tha Carter VI* for selling 108,000 first week units now turning around and calling 90,000 a success. Clipse's 2002 debut album, *Lord Willin'*, scored 122,000 first week sales.

When the smoke cleared, *Let God Sort Em Out* ended up with 118,000 units in its first week, coming within a hair of where they landed for their debut. This led many of the pages to go back on their negative opinions to declare the album a unanimous success.

And all along, the music on the record remained the same.

The Art of the Album Rollout

In 2024, box trucks appeared on the streets of London with chartreuse screens reading "Charli xcx sextape" and her now-husband George's name on them. A "*Brat* wall" was erected in Greenpoint with different messages on it. A viral music video starring an It girl squad including Chloë Sevigny, Julia Fox, and Rachel Sennott was released. A raucous Boiler Room party received a record-breaking 25,000 RSVPs. That night, Charli xcx DJed and hyped up the crowd while wearing an instantly iconic shirt with "CULT CLASSIC" emblazoned on the front. A TikTok dance for "Apple" took the world by storm. Carefully curated remixes arrived with Addison Rae, Robyn, Yung Lean, and, most notably, an internet-breaking turn by Lorde.

The rollout for *Brat* was remarkably self-referential and meta, with Charli even sharing a list of possible marketing ideas she had received that ranged from "Charli gets her nipples pierced at Claire's" to "Charli gets caught shoplifting at the mall and leaks the CCTV footage." A year earlier, Charli had dropped an iconic line about being mood-board fodder on "Speed Drive," a frenetic single from the *Barbie* soundtrack. Back then, she was only a small part of a colour-centric cultural phenomenon. With the release of *Brat*, the tables turned, and Charli was suddenly the one leading the PowerPoint presentation. A multi-pronged cross-cultural assault on every level of media, the rollout for Charli xcx's *Brat* will be studied for years to come. *Brat* is what happens when an auteur is given a budget and the catbird seat in the boardroom.

When Sam Pringle, one of her managers, was interviewed by *Billboard* about the album, he said that Charli provided her team with "a 20-page PDF breaking down every element of *Brat* in full." During this epic months-long rollout that would have felt obnoxious in less capable hands, Charli publicly spelled out the concept behind her album in subtle ways. For some, it started with her private Instagram page @360_brat. Her finsta functioned as a mood board featuring themes from the upcoming album, including song snippets. It was a brilliant way of identifying hardcore fans, early adopters, and influencers who would be most likely to build buzz about her mysterious next release. On January 25th, she tweeted, "everything i do is an extension of my art."

In a March 1st interview on TikTok with Kareem Rahma of SubwayTakes, she shocked the internet by claiming that "music is not important" because "a great artist to me is more than the songs; it's the entire culture and space that they inhabit." Looking back, this was foreshadowing for Charli's world-building approach on *Brat*, making it one of the first albums where the real-world events surrounding its release were consciously designed to feed into and embolden the actual recordings themselves.

"Apple" has a chorus about driving to the airport, which is the location for the "Von dutch" video. Ribald bonus track "Guess" has Charli describing her pink underwear, the same colour she wears in the provocative single art for "360." Charli features Swedish icons Robyn and Yung

Lean on the remix for that song, and their music videos are featured on TV screens in the background of the promo clip for the original track. She playfully references their shared history as child stars on the remix.

Sweden holds significance for Charli: Her first big hit was with Swedish duo Icona Pop, and "Apple" was written there while she stayed with the couple who inspired the song "I think about it all the time." This type of thematic consistency is the hallmark of a complete artistic vision and has become absolutely crucial to extend the life of an album in today's music streaming architecture, which is ravenous for new content and uninterested in encouraging deep listening.

Brat turned out to be an album that explores the rich territory between high and low art with no judgment, a singular effort where Charli bravely cannonballed into the trash, coming up for air with her hands filled with treasure. *Brat* was nominated for the Mercury Prize, hit the number one spot on the U.K. charts, and received a nod for Album of the Year at the Grammys, where she won for Best Dance/Electronic Album and Best Recording Package. Could any of this have been achieved without Charli xcx and her team crafting what I consider to be the greatest and most successful album rollout in history?

▶

Before the twenty-first century, the album rollout as we know it today didn't really exist. An artist would do press interviews at major outlets, maybe perform on television, hope that one of their singles connected on FM radio, and then head out on tour to spread the word in person. In the '80s, the advent of MTV made music videos a key part of the album promotion cycle with efforts such as the John Landis–directed clip for Michael Jackson's "Thriller" boosting album sales to previously unseen levels.

There were certainly promotional happenings related to albums before the modern era. Ahead of the highly anticipated 1976 release of Stevie Wonder's magnum opus *Songs in the Key of Life*, Wonder had "We're almost finished!" shirts made to poke fun at Motown about the album's delays. When the album was complete, the press was summoned to 143-acre Long View Farm Studios in North Brookfield, Massachusetts, to snack on roast beef and champagne as Stevie himself played his album for them on a reel-to-reel tape machine while wearing a full cowboy outfit, complete with a leather fringe jacket. All done to the tune of more than US$170,000 in today's money. A bit like how Kanye West launched his album *Ye* at his ranch in Wyoming, except back in the day, an event like Stevie's wasn't designed for public consumption. Labels and artists didn't see the promotional value of sharing something like this with the audience. Livestreaming over the internet didn't exist yet.

In the past two decades, the album rollout has evolved with artists becoming more openly self-aware about the fact that they are, in fact, promoting a record. They've included fans in the release process in response to technological factors as well as existential threats to the music industry.

Trent Reznor was arguably the first musician to see how real-world actions could filter back to social media, harnessing fan excitement as a means of promoting an album. The *Year Zero* rollout in 2007 was elaborate even by today's standards. It began with a Nine Inch Nails tour shirt featuring a hidden message that spelled out *iamtryingtobelieve*; an enterprising fan added *.com* to the phrase, leading them and other NIN fans to uncover a byzantine "alternate reality game," produced by 42 Entertainment, involving emails, dozens of websites, phone numbers, and more to draw them further into the dystopian world of the game and the album.

Reznor and crew left USB sticks in restrooms for fans to find at their European tour stops that included unreleased songs from the album and clues for the game. The most passionate fans who created art inspired by the game were rewarded with a private NIN show. Reznor activated his audience and used all the tools available to him during that nascent period of the internet to make *Year Zero* feel bigger than just another album release, especially at a time when the music industry was in free fall due to filesharing.

In 2013, Ye successfully leveraged the value in turning the album rollout into a real-world event to draw attention back to the music. The unconventional *Yeezus* rollout began with Ye projecting a stark minimalist video, resembling an art installation, of him performing "New Slaves" at sixty-six locations around the world, giving people the opportunity to hear the song for the first time all at once. I remember attending one of these screenings in Montréal, my body coursing with the sheer excitement of experiencing a one-time-only happening simultaneously with other listeners worldwide. The song itself was uncompromising, raw, and provocative, the urgency of the release method matching the music perfectly.

This moment elicited a collective consciousness feeling that has become fleetingly rare in the intervening years, now reserved for tentpole events like the Super Bowl and the Oscars. *Yeezus* debuted at number one on the *Billboard* 200. The aforementioned 2016 Yeezy season three fashion show that doubled as a Madison Square Garden listening party for *The Life of Pablo* was also culturally significant as part of a similarly unorthodox rollout, but public events for his subsequent albums received comparatively diminished public interest.

This might be related to the paradigm shift sparked by surprise album releases by Beyoncé and David Bowie in 2013, prefigured by Radiohead's pay-what-you-want *In Rainbows* release in 2007. Suddenly, for artists of a certain vintage with a large enough fanbase, it was more impactful to drop a new album on an unsuspecting public without any advance warning, the element of surprise helping the artists elude the album leaks that had become common. Resistance to this approach began to bubble up after U2 forced *Songs of Innocence* into the iTunes libraries of 500 million users in 2014, horrifying many.

The surprise release strategy reached an inflection point with Frank Ocean's masterful gambit of dropping *Blonde* independently the day after *Endless* to fulfill his contract with Def Jam in 2016. From that point on, sudden album drops became so common that they were widely expected, dampening their impact. It was only truly effective for bigger artists. This trend also dovetailed with the rise of Spotify and the decline of music piracy in the 2010s. As the music industry stabilized due to streaming revenue, the surprise release became unremarkable.

In a 2020 interview with *Music Ally*, then Spotify CEO Daniel Ek set out controversial new rules of engagement for artists who want to succeed in the streaming era: "You can't record music once every three to four years and think that's going to be enough. The artists today that are making it realize that it's about creating a continuous engagement with their fans. . . . It is about putting the work in, about the storytelling around the album, and about keeping a continuous dialogue with your fans."

But even as surprise drops had less impact, the early pandemic years had publications like *Vulture* asking "Did 2020 Kill the Long, Fancy Pop-Album Rollout for Good?" At the turn of the decade, attention spans had shrunk. The public's appetite for long, drawn-out rollouts had declined. Putting on a public event with a human audience in the real world wasn't possible for several years. Artists and labels were realizing that they could eschew the costs of a traditional rollout and leverage their massive social media followings to reach their fanbases, who themselves were being trained to consume and exhaust releases with greater speed by the streaming companies.

Former Spotify chief economist Will Page was quoted in a 2024 *Music Radar* report as saying that "more music is being released today (in a single day) than was released in the calendar year of 1989." In 2023, music tracking company Luminate stated that 120,000 new tracks were released on digital service providers every day. Beyond oversaturation on the streaming apps, artists are also competing for eyeballs on social media, elbowing out room against giant corporations, celebrities, and influencers. Regular people have also been incentivized to turn themselves into online creators in the face of Twitch, X, Meta, and TikTok monetizing their social media posting.

A proper rollout can help you break through the noise, which has been getting exponentially louder each year. But most lower- and middle-class musicians don't have the massive budgets required for the attention-grabbing stunts involved in successful album rollouts, especially as the economic gap between the superstars and the rest of us has widened even further in the streaming era. Today's rollouts require several things working in tandem: a creative director who understands the artist and the project, a label that supports and buys into the vision, and a team able to correctly execute the plan and adapt to an ever-changing social environment.

I've tried my hand at album rollouts to varying levels of success. For my first four albums, I did traditional press campaigns. Some of it worked; some of it didn't. But ultimately, I didn't enjoy that part of releasing an album. Making the music was creative and expressive; performing it was cathartic and communal. Promoting a record often felt like a chore.

For my fifth album, *Parallel World*, I connected with creative director Scott Pilgrim (yes, that's what he goes by) back in October 2020. I emailed him with my vision for the album, which had been recorded but hadn't been mixed or mastered yet. I included a mood board of visual references, artists whose conceptual consistency I appreciated during their rollouts: Caroline Polachek, Marie Davidson, and Toro y Moi. I also cited Yung Lean, Ye's *Yeezus* era, and Jay-Z's *4:44* rollout as inspirations.

Scott and I went on to collaborate on the album artwork, merch, music videos, my website, and art direction. We created a social media calendar and planned out posts weeks ahead of time. I made an "Album Bible" on Google Docs with all the themes I explored on *Parallel World*, including things that I read, watched, or listened to that inspired the record, a useful resource to go back to when doing interviews. I treated the rollout like another outlet for my creativity and had fun with it. I also had some politically charged tweets that went viral, further reinforcing the themes of the album.

I started a Substack newsletter and wrote essays about the individual songs, including references and further reading. Having had my work misinterpreted in the past, I was determined to leave no doubt about my intentions this time around. It was a tremendous amount of work, and it certainly required a not-insignificant amount of time and money, but all that world-building paid off: Listeners understood the context of the album more clearly than any of my previous releases. The album won the 2021 Polaris Music Prize, something I partly attribute to its rollout.

On my 2024 follow-up, *Rollercoaster*, I didn't work with a creative director, thinking that maybe I could save money and handle those responsibilities myself. The result was a bit more haphazard. I recorded the album before my son was born in October 2023 and released it when he was six months old. My capacity for making bonus material was severely limited. I worked with photographers Jodi Heartz and Alex Blouin for the visuals, and the project was art directed by Principal. I hired someone to help with social media as well as PR in the U.S., U.K., and Canada. In retrospect, I needed more logistical support with certain aspects of the rollout.

When the album came out in April 2024, it didn't cut through the noise as well as *Parallel World* had. There are creative reasons for this, as the album was a somewhat polarizing musical departure from the record preceding it. But the world had also changed. No longer was I trying to reach a captive audience of content-starved folks stuck at home during the pandemic. People were fully outside again, and social media apps had made it more difficult to promote my work by throttling artists' reach and censoring our output. The traditional music publications had simultaneously become more exclusive and less impactful. I was unable to adapt to the changes in real time.

In this present moment, a well-executed rollout is one of the most effective ways of adapting to our constantly shifting social environment. Superstars like Taylor Swift and the Weeknd are among those who have elevated the rollout to an art form in recent years. Cardi B has received plaudits for the grassroots nature of her rollout for 2025's *Am I the Drama?* She was seen in videos selling copies of her album on the streets of New York like an old-school Canal Street mixtape merchant and hawking CDs out of a candy box to commuters on the subway in the manner of an unsigned rapper.

This methodology stood out for how it spoke to a past familiar to New Yorkers of a certain age who could still remember copping an album directly from the rapper who made it. Cardi threw a pop-up event at Cloud Deli in Washington Heights that took on the bustling atmosphere of a block party as part of the music video shoot for "Bodega Baddie." She gave out two hundred of her favourite deli sandwiches to those who attended, leveraging her star power to draw a massive crowd of real fans for an impressive promotional effort; it simultaneously referenced her New York roots and plopped the superstar in the middle of a real-world happening.

▶

On March 14, 2024, Charli xcx tweeted, "i think the constant demand for access to women's bodies and faces in our album artwork is misogynistic and boring." Every Charli album leading up to *Brat* prominently featured her image on it. Charli had the artwork changed for her complete discography on every music streaming app to coincide with the *Brat* release, extending her album rollout even to administrative decisions. These covers mirrored the omnipresent typography used for the album: glitchy, intentionally pixelated lowercase black Arial text spelling out the album title, superimposed on a puke-green background.

The look became viral. A *Brat* meme generator was created in response to the memes organically popping up online. Charli's tweet revealed that what initially seemed to be a somewhat beguiling cover choice was in fact one with a strong sense of intentionality, a radical decision during an algorithmic era that begs for our faces, lest our posts be relegated to the shadow realm.

Creative directed by Imogene Strauss and designed by Special Offer, designer Brent David Freaney told the *New York Times* that the artwork was the result of a "five-month-long design process" where they looked at "500 different shades of green" before making their decision. The cover is evocative of the indie sleaze era that Charli seeks to valorize with *Brat*, embodying the spirit of the bygone 2000s period when maximalism reigned, scenes and genres freely commingled, and the party felt like it might never end. A time when it seemed as if the entire world was "ready to Uff."

It was around that time that Charli had been discovered as a teen on Myspace. Her parents would drive her to raves to perform. You could see her natural comfort in these environments during her *Brat*-era city-stopping performances at the Lot Radio and Boiler Room. These events helped to position Charli as more than just a pop star. She was a curatorial presence who was tapped in with underground club culture and the authenticity that comes along with it.

Brat felt like a deliberate shift back to her rave roots after 2022's *Crash*, which seemed like a conceptual exercise—what might happen if Charli made a regular, capital-P pop album?—glistening with hits like "Good Ones" and "Beg for You." But in my mind, her last few mainstream releases have lived in the shadow of her 2017 mixtape *Pop 2*. This wildly eclectic collaboration with producer A.G. Cook (who is the Giorgio Moroder to her Donna Summer) was the truest representation of the duality of Charli xcx, emerging after the career reset that was the SOPHIE-produced *Vroom Vroom* EP. Along with *Number 1 Angel*, these three releases documented the conflict between being a literal child of the underground and one of our generation's greatest pop songwriters, someone with all the tools that should lead to superstardom but for whatever reasons hadn't reached it until *Brat*.

The albums that followed the mixtapes seemed to be reaching for the provocative edge of *Pop 2* while firmly keeping a foot in the mainstream pop world. The hedging made them feel compromised. To give you an idea of how she was perceived in the mainstream pre-*Brat*, a 2023 *New York Times* piece entitled "What Happens When a Pop Star Isn't That Popular?" included Charli as a case study.

That tension between mainstream pop and art pop is also at the heart of *Brat*, but the balance has never been better in Charli's career. The album zips by, confidently bouncing across the entire spectrum of pop music from the last few decades. "360," "Apple," and "Von dutch" are conceptually tied to the album's themes but stand on their own as some of her greatest pure pop songs.

Brat often finds Charli revelling in her growing influence on the pop world, which has become progressively harder and harder to ignore, especially in light of records like Camila Cabello's *C,XOXO* appearing on the scene a few weeks after *Brat*. Following *Brat*'s release, the album title practically became a way of life, an ethos unto itself. "Brat summer" was a trend that was bandied about. Charli hosted and performed on *Saturday Night Live*, her rendition of "360" done with heavy Auto-Tune while rocking a vintage 1989 Lou Reed *New York* t-shirt and toting a

Gucci Jackie handbag. *Collins English Dictionary* made "brat" its 2024 word of the year.

In a *Billboard* cover story, Charli was quoted as saying, "I like the marketing of pop music more than I am interested in actual pop music." The marketing and design worlds certainly took notice of her rollout: *The Drum* celebrated how Charli's extensive world-building strategy "recognizes that we all now live in a fractured world mediated and somewhat woven together by the social web," while *Wallpaper** gave the rollout a 2025 Design Award, noting the *Brat* wall in particular as "a masterclass in the deployment of real space with the aim of occupying virtual space."

In July 2024, Charli tweeted "kamala IS brat" in reference to the Democratic presidential nominee, inspiring Harris to reference the aesthetic in her campaign. This also caused Jake Tapper to utter the words "I will aspire to be 'brat'" live on CNN. It's unsurprising to me that the *Brat* rollout resonated with Kamala's team and attracted a rare level of mainstream press for a musician. After all, another way of saying *rollout* is by referring to it as a campaign.

One of the goals of a political campaign, according to Survey & Ballot Systems, is to help potential voters "familiarize themselves with each candidate's style and personality." For the xcx brain trust, the goal was likely to crystallize Charli's identity for the public beyond her established base of gay men, straight women, and electronic music nerds. Instead of votes, the *Brat* campaign was on the hunt for likes and sales, follows and streams.

On the *Tape Notes* podcast, Charli and her producers George Daniel and A.G. Cook discussed how something being in "*Brat* world" or not figured into their creative process while making the album. Similar to other great British poets of the club, like Soft Cell's Marc Almond and Neil Tennant of the Pet Shop Boys, who mined the elegiac sadness lurking around the edges of nightlife, Charli expertly captures the vulnerability and fallibility that lies behind the party girl persona she has cultivated. She cements herself as someone with great familiarity with the twisted dream logic of the rave, where a night starts in the morning and you go to sleep when the sun is up.

One notable influence on *Brat* is the Streets, a.k.a. Mike Skinner, whom she references on "Club classics." Skinner himself once bragged about being "cult classic, not bestseller" and explored the darkness hidden beneath the mirror balls and lights with stunning specificity, elevating the mundane details of the rave to operatic levels in the process. Charli's pen is exacting: biting character study "Mean girls" is reminiscent of fellow auteur Grace Jones on songs such as "Party Girl."

Penultimate track "I think about it all the time," a delicately sweet song about considering parenthood, is immediately contrasted by brash album closer "365," a sped-up reimagining of "360" where Charli goes full-on party monster, ripping lines of blow and spewing a depraved rave mantra: "Don't sleep, don't eat, just do it on repeat." Similar to Kendrick Lamar on *Mr. Morale & the Big Steppers*, Charli doesn't care if the listener still likes her by the end of the album. It's an ego-destroying forty-one minutes that resembles actual self-reflection, eschewing the therapy-speak, trauma porn, and superficial gestures offered by many of today's mainstream artists for a warts-and-all look at pop star anxiety.

What was it about the *Brat* rollout that worked so well? Charli was totally herself in all her messy, irreverent glory throughout the whole process. Everything that happened over the course of the campaign felt like a real moment, and Charli never seemed to take herself or her changing circumstances too seriously. It became nearly impossible to know where the rollout ended and her life began, her every move a kind of performance, and the audience was captivated.

Her album release strategy stands in opposition to Daniel Ek's cynical advice for today's artists. Charli's *Brat* era treated her album like a living, breathing organism, not just something to drop unceremoniously before moving on to your second or third release of the year. Similar to how a successful political campaign runs, her team was incredibly adept at reacting rapidly to the outside world's engagement and seized opportunities with a precision that hadn't been seen before in the world of music.

▶

We've reached the point where we're seeing album release strategies that are clearly informed by *Brat*'s. Lorde's campaign for *Virgin* in 2025 was arguably the first great post-*Brat* album rollout. Like Charli, she started by connecting with her most diehard fans: Lorde solicited phone numbers through an app called Community, which allowed her to text her audience directly. Over the ensuing weeks, superfans were treated to song snippets, a tour announcement, and iPhone voice notes of Lorde rambling about her forthcoming record, which had me rapt in anticipation.

Lorde invited her fans to Washington Square Park in New York on April 22, 2025. After the amassed crowd was broken up by the police, she appeared a couple hours later to dance along to her single "What Was That" being blasted from a speaker dragged there by Blood Orange's Dev Hynes. The video for the song arrived two days later, filmed with an iPhone to cultivate a mood of authentic intimacy. Footage from the aforementioned real-world happening ended up as the centrepiece of the video, as Lorde emerged from a fake sewer hole to join the unsuspecting crowd in the park.

Leveraging something that happened in real life as an intentional part of an album rollout wasn't the only *Brat*-like technique used by Lorde. Like a rapper in a war of words with a rival emcee, Charli kept people talking about *Brat* through tweets shading Camila Cabello as well as posts stoking fan speculation that she had written songs about both Lorde and Taylor Swift on her album. Lorde similarly brought attention back to *Virgin* through public statements, setting off a minor bit of controversy when she said that she watched the Tommy Lee and Pamela Anderson sex tape and found it "beautiful" in a cover story interview for *Rolling Stone*. This somewhat random admission was met with confusion and furor on social media with some taking issue that she would intentionally watch a sex tape that exploited the participants against their will as well as her suggestion that Pamela and Tommy "were like children" in it.

All of this was mostly forgotten by the time *Virgin* was released. The context of the Tommy and Pamela reference was clarified on album standout "Current Affairs"; she sings about the couple and the tape in a more nuanced, artful way than she spoke about them in the *Rolling Stone* interview. The brief controversy mostly served the purpose of reminding the public that Lorde was back and had a new album on the way, all while taking advantage of the rapid churn of the internet's outrage cycle and functioning as a callback to the album itself.

The metallic Thom Browne outfit she wore to the Met Gala foreshadowed the duct tape she covered her chest with in the "Man of the Year" music video. *Virgin*'s themes of vulnerability, self-reflection, gender, and transparency are referenced in various ways, from the X-ray of her body and clear PVC clothing in the album artwork to her confessional interviews during the rollout to the use of mirrors in press photos.

A release campaign like this can be inspiring. It signals that the artist believes enough in this particular record to pull out all the stops and commit themselves fully, to make all the gruelling behind-the-scenes considerations required to ensure the trail of breadcrumbs leads somewhere satisfying.

But what happens when all that planning backfires? Enter Katy Perry. Her rollout for *143* will be remembered as one of the worst of all time.

Confounding debut single "Woman's World" found Perry reconnecting with producer Dr. Luke, known in recent years for sexual assault allegations levelled against him by former collaborator Kesha. A forgettable, limp electro-pop number, the song's contradictory women's lib message was roundly panned; a one-star *Guardian* review asked, "What regressive, warmed-over hell is this?"

The bizarre video for "Woman's World" features Perry dressed as Rosie the Riveter, suggestively pouring a bottle of whiskey all over herself. Later on, she marches to a gas station while wearing robot legs and sticks a gas-pump nozzle into her butt cheek, for some reason. Seemingly going for camp surrealism while aiming to simultaneously promote girl power and satisfy the male gaze, Katy Perry fails at it all. Amazingly, this wasn't even the worst part of the rollout.

While shooting the video for follow-up single "Lifetimes," Perry was accused of illegally filming in S'Espalmador of the Balearic Islands, a protected ecological location in Spain known for its sand dunes that doesn't allow visitors without proper accreditation. In a statement, Perry's team claimed that they were given "verbal approval" to shoot there and had gotten the proper permits for filming in Spain, but the one for that specific location was still "in process." This debacle signalled just how ill-prepared and underdeveloped the *143* rollout was. Each mistake snowballed until the album's failure felt preordained.

Released September 20, 2024, *143* was pelted with negative reviews on a worldwide scale. Review aggregator Metacritic gave the album a combined score of thirty-seven out of one hundred, making it the lowest scoring album of the decade so far and the nineteenth worst-rated album since the website started in 2001. British *GQ* put it best with the headline "Katy Perry's Anti-*Brat* Album Rollout Is Cursed."

If an album rollout is similar to a political campaign, Katy Perry would be the Jeb Bush to Charli's Obama. It would be enough to make someone want to leave Earth, which she literally did as part of a Blue Origin sub-orbital space flight, another poorly received promotional effort. A struggle with authenticity doomed the forever-polished yet uncanny Perry, her complete lack of self-awareness putting her firmly out of step with the times.

▶

A rollout that goes on for too long can result in the initial hype dissipating over time. The interminable length of ASAP Rocky's rollout for *Don't Be Dumb* turned the album into a punchline in hip-hop circles. His previous release, *Testing*, came out all the way back in 2018. He began teasing the follow-up in December 2022 when he announced the title at a show during 2 Chainz's Amazon Music Live series. In an August 2024 *Billboard* cover story, he claimed to have played the unreleased album for Tim Burton, and the *Edward Scissorhands* director was "fucking with it heavy." (Tim Burton went on to design the *Don't Be Dumb* album cover and star in the music video for "WHISKEY/BLACK DEMARCO".) But even after releasing several singles complete with videos over the following year, *Don't Be Dumb* was pushed back time and time again. Rocky blamed sample clearances and leaks. He also dealt with a pair of high profile legal cases between albums: an assault charge in Sweden he was convicted for that put him in prison for a month and a gun charge in Los Angeles that he beat that was lobbed at him by a former A$AP member.

In a *GQ* interview during the press junket for his film *Highest 2 Lowest*, Spike Lee pointedly asked when the album was coming, and a slightly rattled Rocky demurred, saying, "I'ma just drop it. I don't wanna say another date [and] disappoint people," eventually claiming that the album was "done." He subsequently sold a hoodie emblazoned with the words "ALBUM NEVER DROPPING" at the 2025 edition of

Camp Flog Gnaw. With each successive delay, the potency of *Don't Be Dumb's* eventual release was weakened.

As the months continued to roll by, Rocky infuriated a fanbase used to the more truncated rollouts exhibited by artists like Tyler, the Creator. (*Don't Be Dumb* was finally released to great fanfare on January 16, 2026, debuting at the top spot on the Billboard 200.) Unlike the unfocused, halting *Don't Be Dumb* rollout, Tyler the Creator is a modern master of the rollout; there's no one better in the world of rap at activating their audience when it's time to put out a new release. *Chromakopia* was announced with no prior buildup, slated for an unusual Monday release on October 28, 2024. Sepia-toned video clips that recalled *Dr. Strangelove* introduced the new era, with Tyler rocking a strangely angular haircut, a mask of his own face, and military regalia.

Unlike the unfocused, seemingly endless *Don't Be Dumb* rollout, the *Chromakopia* promotional cycle was brief and effective. It delivered on its promise quickly. There were only twelve days between the announcement and the album hitting streaming services; Tyler was surgical with this concise schedule. He followed *Chromakopia* with the rapid-fire, inverted rollout of *Don't Tap the Glass* the next year when he put the previously unannounced album on sale on his website after teasing that something would be coming on July 21, 2025, a week in advance.

▶

Naturally, we have to consider that promoting an album on a *Brat*-like scale requires a certain level of privilege that is largely unavailable to the rank-and-file musicians out there. Indie labels aren't capable of bankrolling the type of think tank required to make these moves. I was only able to try my hand at the low-budget version of a rollout like this because of the support I received from the Canadian arts grant system.

One must also admit that despite how inspiring it is to see an artist empowered by their label and team to make something beyond themselves that resonates with millions, these blockbuster album rollouts take up a lot of oxygen in the media landscape. That's attention that could've been spread out to hundreds of other, smaller artists. Instead, it's centralized in the hands of big-name acts who have access to the best strategists.

By the time the 2025 Grammys came and went in February 2025, *Brat* fatigue was beginning to set in. An end to the campaign looked to be near. In a masterfully meta moment during the second week of Coachella in April, Charli used the screens to ask the audience (and seemingly herself) whether Brat summer was finally over, as potential keepers of the season for the current year suddenly flashed by: Addison Rae, PinkPantheress, Haim, Yung Lean, David Cronenberg, Joachim Trier. In an April 29, 2025, Instagram caption, Charli wrote, "i'm interested in the tension of staying too long," a very *Brat* sentiment in and of itself. A *Brat* retrospective zine was released on June 25th, selling out quickly.

She closed out Glastonbury that month by burning a backdrop with the word *brat* crossed out on it. Soon after, the album artwork for her back catalogue on the streaming apps reverted to the original covers. A mockumentary satirizing the *Brat* rollout called *The Moment*, directed by Aidan Zamiri and starring Charli, premiered at the 2026 Sundance Film Festival and received a wider North American cinematic release on January 30, 2026. When asked whether the film signified the end of the era at a press conference for the 2026 Berlin Film Festival, Charli replied, "For me, it's over."

No one could call it anything but a success. Maintaining relevance around one release for twenty months is a Herculean feat that we might never see again. The rollout reimagined as art installation, Charli xcx's career-defining meta-commentary on the album format will also never be forgotten.

Redemption Songs

In April 2025, Belfast rap group Kneecap shared a message on stage at Coachella: "Israel is committing genocide against the Palestinian people. It is being enabled by the U.S. government who arm and fund Israel despite their war crimes. Fuck Israel, Free Palestine." Pundits on Fox News criticized the band. They received death threats. Their American booking agency, Independent Artist Group, dropped them. Sharon Osbourne called for "the revocation of Kneecap's work visa" on X. Federal MP Vince Gasparro erroneously claimed in a video that the Canadian government had banned the group from the country ahead of their shows in Vancouver and Toronto.

That June, at Glastonbury, Bobby Vylan of U.K. punk rap duo Bob Vylan stepped onstage and chanted, "Death, death to the IDF." Condemnation was swift from every angle of the establishment. U.K. prime minister Keir Starmer called it "appalling hate speech"; the BBC, which broadcast the performance, called it "deeply offensive"; Avon and

Somerset police said that they were investigating the performance as well as that of Kneecap, who also played the festival. Bob Vylan's U.S. visas were revoked, and their booking agency dropped them.

Just like the parental advisory sticker in the '90s, the negative media attention and authoritarian denunciations have only turned Kneecap and Bob Vylan into the hottest, most rebellious acts in the world. Both bands zoomed up the charts after Glastonbury, with Bob Vylan reaching the top spot on the U.K.'s Official Hip Hop and R&B Albums Chart. In the wake of the controversy, their merch was completely sold out. Despite getting dropped by their agent at UTA, Bob Vylan were still booked and busy in the immediate aftermath, with dozens of shows planned for the following months.

In the past, the backlash against Bob Vylan and Kneecap would've been devastating to their careers. But in a social media world, it's no longer possible for the mainstream news media to totally dictate the narrative around what a musician has said. Socially conscious since their inception, Massive Attack have been unflinching and consistent in their advocacy for Palestine. Their moral clarity has led them to start a U.K. artists syndicate with Brian Eno, Fontaines D.C., and Kneecap to combat "aggressive, vexatious campaigns" to "censor and silence artists from speaking their hearts and minds" by pro-Israel entities like UK Lawyers for Israel. Eno was behind the Together for Palestine benefit concert at Wembley Arena, which featured Damon Albarn, Hot Chip, James Blake, King Krule, and more, to raise money for Choose Love, a British charity that collaborates with partner organizations in Gaza to provide medical supplies and food.

In 2023, British rapper Stormzy posted "Free Palestine" on Instagram. That same year, a boycott against McDonald's was organized after Alonyal, owner and operator of all the McDonald's restaurants in Israel, gave away thousands of free meals to the IDF. In early 2024, Stormzy archived his "Free Palestine" post ahead of a McDonald's campaign for the Stormzy Meal in February 2024. He was lambasted by fans. Stormzy claimed that the post was tucked away as part of an unrelated "mass archiving effort" and that his support for Palestine hadn't changed, but his standing with fans has suffered ever since he made this hypocritical brand partnership. In August 2025, Toro y Moi was similarly lambasted for tweeting "that feeling when u finally get to go on ur dream vacation to mcdonaldland #ad," alongside a video of him in the studio recording a McDonald's jingle while jubilantly pouring fries into his mouth.

During an October 2024 show in Melbourne, Thom Yorke left the stage after a fan shouted at him about the death toll in Gaza and asked, "How could you be silent?" Yorke remained quiet for months before sharing a poorly received statement in May 2025 that centred his own personal anxiety, carefully avoided naming Israel, and called out "social media witch-hunts" for "pressurizing artists and whoever they feel like that week to make statements."

Radiohead had been lauded for years as a politically conscious band, so when Yorke came off so out of touch in his statement, it felt like a betrayal to some fans. Rumours swirled that the band's nine-year hiatus was related to a difference of opinion about this subject, though the band has since announced a string of European shows slated for late 2025. Some attributed Yorke's dithering response to his relationship with bandmate Jonny Greenwood, who is married to Israeli visual artist Sharona Katan. Katan wrote an op-ed for *Haaretz* in June 2024 in defence of her husband that denounced the "disgusting campaign to force all Jews outside Israel to proclaim themselves anti-Israel if they wish to remain acceptable in the public eye."

Similar to South African apartheid and its impact on musicians in the '80s, we will all be left with lasting images of how the artists of our time engaged with the topic of Israel and Palestine. Reminiscent of Artists United Against Apartheid in the '80s, over four hundred artists including

Japanese Breakfast, Mogwai, Aminé, and Soccer Mommy joined No Music for Genocide in September 2025, vowing to geo-block their music on streaming services in Israel as a way to "reject political repression, shift public opinion toward justice, and refuse the art-washing and normalization of any company or nation that commits crimes against humanity."

▶

Politically conscious musicians have consistently put their lives and livelihoods at risk to speak truth to power throughout history. Protest music in America is rooted in workers' rights anthems such as "Bread and Roses" and African-American hymns like "Lift Every Voice and Sing," a subversive rallying cry for freedom that became known as the "Black National Anthem." A haunting metaphor for lynching written by Jewish poet and teacher Abel Meeropol, "Strange Fruit" became a rare socially conscious Depression-era jazz track in Billie Holiday's hands. Her label Columbia refused to record the song so she was forced to take it to indie imprint Commodore Records, which released it in 1939.

Southern radio stations banned it from the airwaves, but "Strange Fruit" still ended up selling over a million copies and making it to number sixteen on the *Billboard* charts. Federal Bureau of Narcotics commissioner Harry Anslinger made it his personal mission to destroy Holiday after she refused to stop performing the song, eventually entrapping her with undercover agents who sold her heroin, landing her in prison and stripping her of her cabaret performer's license. She died at the age of forty-four from heart failure related to cirrhosis of the liver, but the legacy of "Strange Fruit" lives on; *Time* magazine called it the song of the century in 1999.

Music's role in identity politics became clearer in the post-war era after the dawn of the record industry made it possible to bring the jazz café back home with you in the form of the vinyl record. White listeners' desire to emulate the self-possessed cool of the original Black jazz hipsters of the 1940s developed not long after, but this mimicry wasn't for political reasons. In Norman Mailer's controversial 1957 essay "The White Negro," he highlights the Western social binary of his time as a clash between the underground and the mainstream: "One is Hip or one is Square . . . one is a rebel or one conforms, one is a frontiersman in the Wild West of American night life, or else a Square cell, trapped in the totalitarian tissues of American society, doomed willy-nilly to conform if one is to succeed."

Figures like Harry Belafonte managed to strike a balance by speaking for the dispossessed while simultaneously crossing over into the public consciousness. His hero was Paul Robeson, the outspoken multi-hyphenate superstar who was blacklisted and banned from leaving the States during the McCarthy era because of his unrelenting public support for Soviet policies. Belafonte is remembered as one of the most socially conscious entertainers of the 1950s.

The National Museum of African American History and Culture's website calls him "instrumental in the Civil Rights Movement." Belafonte helped organize the March on Washington and provided early funding for the Student Nonviolent Coordinating Committee. He literally bailed out student activists from jail. He also helped plan MLK's memorial. But the activist message behind songs like "Day-O (The Banana Boat Song)" wouldn't have been obvious to the casual listener.

I can envision white liberals of the day bragging to their friends about how they went to see a Harry Belafonte picture the same way that Bradley Whitford's villain in Jordan Peele's 2017 Black horror film *Get Out* assures Daniel Kaluuya's protagonist that he would've voted Obama in for a third term if he could have.

At a time when Black people were fighting for equal rights, to be treated as human beings, sentiments like these had to be smuggled in with more subtlety than they would be in later years. Belafonte's humanitarian interests stemmed equally from a natural inclination toward the upward mobility of his fellow Black Americans as from the abject poverty he grew up in. Because of who he was and what he represented throughout the rest of his life, listening to his music became a meaningful act in and of itself, as he thoughtfully explained in his memoir *My Song*: "If you liked Harry Belafonte, you were making a political statement, and that felt good, the way it felt good to listen to Paul Robeson, and hear what he had to say. If you were a white Belafonte fan, you felt even better. You were connecting with your better angels, reaching across the racial divide. Consciously or not, you were casting your vote for equality."

But despite the strides that he made for the advancement of Black people in America, Belafonte's political efforts created problems in his personal life. A critical 1957 piece in famed Black publication *Amsterdam News* claimed that his "popularity with his own race [was] hanging in the balance" for marrying Julie Robinson, a white woman.

In a 1996 *New Yorker* interview in which the entertainer is referred to as "the perfect hybrid of popular culture and political conscience," Belafonte bemoaned the dearth of Black people at his shows and a lack of acceptance from African-American culture at large: "Even before, because of my social and political position, most black people distanced themselves from me. . . . In California, I walked into a place and somebody said, 'Here comes Mr. Conscience,' and all the cocaine left the room—you know?"

In the '60s, Bob Dylan was lauded for his support of the civil rights movement, following in the footsteps of his idol Woody Guthrie, the working-class hero behind "This Land Is Your Land." But not every person who listened to "The Lonesome Death of Hattie Carroll" necessarily understood or agreed with the sentiment behind it. Despite performing on the same stage as Martin Luther King Jr. on the night of his

"I Have a Dream" speech among other politically salient performances throughout this brief politically engaged period of his career, Dylan mostly kept his leanings intentionally vague beyond his protest songs.

Legendary folk singer and Dylan's former partner Joan Baez tried to persuade him to remain involved in politics, but Dylan balked. "The obvious thing was music and politics for me," she explained in the documentary *Joan Baez: I Am a Noise*. Baez walked in the 1965 Montgomery to Selma marches in solidarity with the civil rights movement, sang "We Shall Overcome" at the March on Washington, and started the Institute for the Study of Non-Violence, forever blurring the line between artist and activist.

Dylan once told fellow folk singer Phil Ochs, "The stuff you're writing is bullshit, because politics is bullshit." Like Baez, Ochs stayed the path. Preferring to be called a "topical singer," Phil Ochs consistently spoke to the times on songs like "Talking Cuban Crisis," "Love Me, I'm a Liberal," and "Draft Dodger Rag." During a 1968 protest against the Vietnam War, young men in the crowd started setting their draft cards on fire when he performed his anti-war anthem "I Ain't Marching Any More." His sardonic wit and self-effacing attitude may have limited his commercial prospects, as he never managed to break out of the folk scene and into the mainstream. Ochs died by suicide in 1976 at the age of thirty-five after living with untreated and undiagnosed bipolar disorder and alcoholism.

Nina Simone, a jazz singer and classical pianist who melded the social consciousness of folk with the rawness of the blues and the ecclesiastical fury of gospel, was a chameleonic figure who became synonymous with the civil rights movement through "Mississippi Goddam." The song was banned in some southern states, and one record dealer in South Carolina snapped promo copies of "Mississippi Goddam" in half and shipped the shards back to the label.

In her autobiography *I Put a Spell on You*, Simone explained why she finally relented to the pull of mixing politics with music: "I didn't like 'protest music' because a lot of it was so simple and unimaginative it stripped the dignity away from the people it was trying to celebrate. But the Alabama church bombing and the murder of Medgar Evers stopped that argument and with 'Mississippi Goddam' I realized there was no turning back."

The civil rights movement made it impossible to ignore the treatment of Black Americans at the hands of a systemically racist society and establishment. "A Change Is Gonna Come" by Sam Cooke shows how by the middle of the '60s, Black artists were becoming progressively more open in their songs about their experiences being treated as a lesser class of human being. Inspired by King's "I Have a Dream" speech and Dylan's "Blowin' in the Wind," Cooke wrote about his own brushes with racial prejudice, exposing the American apartheid state fostered by Jim Crow.

Music with a message in the '60s spoke directly to the particularly turbulent times of its creation. Crosby, Stills, Nash & Young called out Nixon by name on "Ohio" and elegized the fleeting hippie era with "Almost Cut My Hair." But some artists were not as explicit about their political perspective. During the time of the Vietnam War, the Kent State shootings, civil rights, and women's rights movements, as well as the assassinations of political figures like John F. Kennedy, Malcolm X, and MLK, many of the groups that became synonymous with the decade, such as the Beatles and the Grateful Dead, were anti-establishment rather than overtly political. The Rolling Stones in particular approached the upheaval of the '60s from a detached perspective in songs like "Street Fighting Man" and "Gimme Shelter."

More direct was James Brown's "Say It Loud—I'm Black and I'm Proud," a 1968 rallying cry from the Godfather of Funk that galvanized the Black Power movement. By the dawn of the '70s, there were Black revolutionary acts like the Last Poets and Gil Scott-Heron who rose from the ashes of the failed utopian promise of the '60s hippie dream and anticipated hip-hop with their rhythmic and poetic salvos. Both groups had ties to the Black Panther Party. Scott-Heron's "The Revolution Will Not Be Televised" was a response song to the Last Poets' "When the Revolution Comes," a synergy that showed their connection to the same struggle. The Last Poets were anti-capitalist in their complete lack of commercial overtures, their unmelodious music not much more than bongos and unflinching social commentary.

Gil Scott-Heron was the kind of poet who could convincingly write a song like "We Almost Lost Detroit" about the 1966 partial meltdown of the Enrico Fermi Nuclear Generating Station on the shore of Lake Erie and then perform it at an event like the No Nukes concerts at Madison Square Garden without coming off as sanctimonious. Along with Stevie Wonder, who took aim at President Nixon on the piercing "You Haven't Done Nothin'," Scott-Heron was a pivotal force behind the campaign to make MLK's birthday a national holiday. Nine of his albums made it to the *Billboard* 200, and he was one of the defining voices of the '70s until substance abuse derailed his career. He died in 2011, a year after issuing his well-received comeback album *I'm New Here*.

Sly and the Family Stone directly responded to Marvin Gaye's searching 1971 exploration of the national psyche *What's Going On* later that year with a searing indictment: *There's a Riot Goin' On*. The interracial rock band eschewed the brighter, pop-friendly tunes of their previous work for a raw, murky dive into unencumbered funk that echoed the fearsome, seemingly hopeless new decade they had just entered.

A reflection of where America was racially at the time, the Black Panthers asked Sly to kick the white members out of his band to no avail. *Riot* captured the mood of the era, as explained in a *New Yorker* retrospective on the album by Hanif Abdurraqib: "The lyrics were not necessarily pessimistic, and they were not all explicitly political, but they were tinged with a kind of cynicism that seemed to be overtaking the country."

Evolving out of mento and ska and influenced by American R&B, reggae was Jamaica's soundtrack to civic unrest, and the genre broke out beyond the island in the '70s with the help of socially conscious artists like Bob Marley. Time has softened much of his message and image, but back then, Marley was a near-messianic figure, a Rastafarian rebel with a cause who crafted timeless protest songs like "Get Up, Stand Up," "Redemption Song," and "I Shot the Sheriff" as his tools to rail against injustice.

His sway with his fellow Jamaicans grew to the point that regional political parties considered him a threat, even allegedly having him and his entourage shot at his residence Tuff Gong to prevent Marley from performing at the Smile Jamaica Concert in 1976. He survived the assassination attempt and still played the event, joining hands with the leaders of the rival political parties at the time, People's National Party and the conservative Jamaican Labour Party, in an effort for unity.

Fela Kuti was Nigeria's answer to James Brown, a bandleader and activist who was the driving force behind Afrobeat, a blistering hybrid of funk, jazz, rock, and traditional African music like Ghanian highlife and Yoruba. He started a political party called Movement of the People but was banned from being a candidate in Nigeria's general election.

His incendiary songs like "Zombie" criticized the Nigerian military, which raided and eventually destroyed his commune, defenestrating his seventy-seven-year-old mother, who would later die from her injuries. Fela, alongside sixty supporters, delivered a ceremonial coffin in honour of his mother to Nigerian head of state headquarters in 1979, as commemorated on "Coffin for Head of State." His dedication to political causes actively hindered his life, causing him to be arrested and beaten by police more than once, but he never stopped advocating through his music.

In the U.K., Linton Kwesi Johnson's dub poetry turned him into the Windrush generation's answer to Gil Scott-Heron. He sharply criticized racial injustice on songs like "It Dread inna Inglan," which was dedicated to George Lindo, a Black man who was wrongly imprisoned for robbery. Around the same time, the Clash were in West London crystallizing punk's potential for social justice with reggae-inflected songs that focused on sociopolitical issues.

Joe Strummer shared the band's manifesto with *NME* in 1976: "I think people ought to know that we're anti-fascist, we're anti-violence, we're anti-racist and we're pro-creative." Among the first groups to wear their politics on their sleeve through their use of militaristic dress as a provocative fashion statement, Strummer saw the value of connecting sound with aesthetic early on, quoted by punk zine *Sniffin' Glue* saying, "like trousers, like brain."

The commingling of altruism, art, and commerce would complicate the purity of political efforts by musicians at the dawn of the next decade. During the '80s, musicians supported major causes that also doubled as massive branding opportunities for themselves. Events like Live Aid, Farm Aid, and Hands Across America; groups like Artists United Against Apartheid; and collaborative songs like "Do They Know It's Christmas?" and "We Are the World" (the latter organized by Harry Belafonte) became emblematic of the decade, as celebrities and musicians banded together to raise money for charity in front of a worldwide audience (though the value of these fundraisers was, in retrospect, limited).

Bruce Springsteen emerged from Freehold, New Jersey, in the late '70s to become "the voice of the working class" by the end of the '80s, mining the minutiae of small-town life for decade-defining success that flew in the face of Wall Street extravagance. Neil Young, socially conscious over the course of his career, organized Farm Aid with Willie Nelson and John Mellencamp in 1985, raising over $9 million for American family farmers, and he struck out against the commercialism of the decade with "This Note's for You."

U2 made social consciousness a part of their brand from the outset of their career in the early '80s. From singing about the Troubles on "Sunday Bloody Sunday" to linking up with Greenpeace to protest the Sellafield nuclear plant, U2 and Bono in particular never missed an opportunity to use their platform to advocate for various causes. What would normally be worth celebrating grew cloying over time. Bono's sanctimonious earnestness and his hopelessly broad lyrics took on a bumper-sticker quality with each successive album. "I wonder if the fact that they are still at it is too much to bear for some, that they are still wrestling out loud with and awash in the contradictions of wealth and consciousness," wrote David Dark in an essay for *America Magazine*.

As their collective net worth grew to obscene levels, fans could sense an inverse weakening in the power of their message. Whatever good Bono has brought into the world through his countless philanthropic efforts is now seen as little more than an ego exercise by many. He's become the model for the activist musician, an example of what can happen if you centre yourself too much in your advocacy as an artist.

Fellow Irish artist Sinéad O'Connor was critical of U2, derisively calling them "bombastic" in a 1987 *i-D* magazine interview, later accusing Bono of "faking that sincerity." O'Connor had a naturally oppositional personality that was reflected in her confrontational image—a head shaved bald and Doc Martens—as well as in her uncompromising pop music that unexpectedly resonated with a large audience when she arrived on the international scene in the late '80s. No one else looked or sounded like her, and few artists were as free with their opinions.

Her outspoken nature caused controversies. Her refusal to have "The Star-Spangled Banner" played before a 1990 show in New Jersey led to calls for her music to be censored. When she ripped up a photo of Pope

John Paul II on *Saturday Night Live* during an a cappella performance of Bob Marley's "War" in 1992 to protest child sexual abuse in the Catholic Church, she was met with worldwide derision. A group known as the National Ethnic Coalition of Organizations got a steamroller to crush hundreds of her albums outside the office of her label, Chrysalis Records. She was blacklisted by the music industry and her career never recovered, striking fear into the hearts of other musicians who might hope to avoid her fate.

Other politically minded artists around this time were also subject to censorship. Having grown up on the Last Poets, Public Enemy were fearless in marrying the Bomb Squad's jarring, dystopian production with the uncommonly anti-establishment lyrics of Chuck D and Flavor Flav, making them early flag-bearers for political rap. The group was chiefly responsible for the popularization of Afrocentric fashion and attitudes in the African-American community in the '90s. Public Enemy's dissonantly funky songs, charged with danger and urgency, helped rap be seen as a serious art form capable of significant social commentary, proving that hip-hop music was the ultimate vehicle for political sentiments in the process.

The group's image was stained by homophobic and antisemitic statements to the press made by nonperforming member Professor Griff in 1989. (Perhaps this all could've been avoided if they never had a "Minister of Information" in their rap group in the first place.) The controversy caused Chuck D to threaten to disband the group ahead of "Fight the Power" and their landmark album *Fear of a Black Planet*. Much like the b-boy in their famous logo, being a political rap group placed them in the crosshairs of increased media scrutiny.

That same target logo was drawn on the side of Sinéad O'Connor's head during her performance of "Mandinka" at the 1989 Grammy Awards. She rocked it in solidarity with Public Enemy and the entire hip-hop community who had been ignored by the institution for years, despite making some of the most culturally significant music of the time. It was the first year with a Best Rap Performance category, but the award wouldn't be televised. Nominees Salt-N-Pepa, LL Cool J, and DJ Jazzy Jeff & the Fresh Prince boycotted the ceremony.

In a 1990 interview with *Rolling Stone*, Sinéad O'Connor told reporter Mikal Gilmore that hip-hop was the genre that she believed has "the closest spiritual kinship to her own music." O'Connor didn't show up to the 1991 Grammys where she was nominated for four awards and sent a letter instead, accusing the music industry of having "false and destructive materialistic values." Public Enemy boycotted the awards alongside her; the rap category was not televised yet again. That same night, Vernon Reid of Living Colour went up to the podium to accept his award for Best Hard Rock Performance sporting a white sleeveless shirt with Sinéad's face on it.

Following on the heels of N.W.A.'s "Fuck tha Police" in 1989, countless rappers during hip-hop's golden age of the '90s referenced police brutality in the wake of Rodney King's beating as well as rhymed about other social issues. But the rise of Bad Boy Records and the "bling bling" era led to a period of conspicuous consumption and rampant consumerism, which went on to define rap into the new century.

Underground bands such as Bikini Kill and Fugazi kept things political. The Beastie Boys organized Tibetan Freedom Concerts with the Milarepa Fund. Welsh group Manic Street Preachers deeply embedded sociopolitical issues into each of their albums with track titles like "If You Tolerate This Your Children Will Be Next," "Let Robeson Sing," and "Ifwhiteamericatoldthetruthforonedayit'sworldwouldfallapart." Fellow U.K. band Radiohead developed a reputation for being politically conscious through songs like "Electioneering" and, most notably, the George W. Bush–skewering *Hail to the Thief*. And Massive Attack rose to fame in the '90s, one of the only bands I've seen whose "Activism and politics" section on Wikipedia is nearly longer than the one about their music.

But in the '90s, there was no bigger political group than Rage Against the Machine. Their self-titled debut melded Tom Morello's metal-infused guitar wizardry with the socially conscious rhymes and chants of vocalist Zack De La Rocha and featured a photograph of the self-immolation of Vietnamese protester Thích Quảng Đức on its cover. It's likely the only album to thank both Black Panther Huey P. Newton and Provisional IRA hunger striker Bobby Sands for inspiration in the liner notes.

This was rap-rock that spiritually followed in the footsteps of Public Enemy's "Bring the Noise" collaboration with Anthrax. A *Los Angeles Times* piece by Robert Hilburn covering their 1993 Lollapalooza set described De La Rocha onstage as being a combination of "Chuck D.'s accessibility and power as a rapper with Bob Marley's determination as a performer." In the same piece, Hilburn noted how '90s rock bands and fans seemed reluctant to mix music with politics, "disillusioned perhaps by the way they see their parents' generation failing to live up to the lofty ideals of '60s rock."

By the turn of the century, the flame of protest music had largely been snuffed out. Rage Against the Machine broke up in 2000, which, according to Ann Powers in a piece for the *New York Times*, "seemed to deal yet another crushing blow to the notion that self-defined activist artists could succeed." Mainstream hip-hop was content to let the party rage on, outside of dead prez, OutKast, Lupe Fiasco, Yasiin Bey, and figures from the underground rap scene like Immortal Technique and the Coup.

There was a sprinkling of dissent in punk from bands like Propagandhi as well as some anti-Bush sentiment, such as on Green Day's "American Idiot." System of a Down protested the Iraq war with "Boom!" and "B.Y.O.B.," and the Chicks were banned from country music stations for Natalie Maines's critical statements about Bush's involvement in that conflict, subsequently responding to the controversy with "Not Ready to Make Nice."

But any expectation that the multiple wars, terror attacks, Hurricane Katrina, and other assorted upheavals of the early twenty-first century might result in a new golden age for protest music was misplaced. The resistance was not as centralized as it once was, despite there being no lack of relevant subject matter. We were no longer reading the same newspapers or watching the same television programs. Our media diets had become hopelessly stratified by the internet, our activities more individualistic than ever before.

The dearth of protest music in the 2000s could also be attributed to more cautious major labels that were less likely to rock the boat with their signings after filesharing nearly brought the music industry to its knees. For some artists, perhaps the calculus became similar to Michael Jordan's infamous "Republicans buy sneakers too" joke from when he was asked why he didn't endorse Democratic candidate Harvey Gantt for North Carolina senate in 1990.

Where were the young protest singers? Where had the rabble-rousers gone? The spirit of resistance slowly reemerged in the 2010s, right as hip-hop regained its natural place as the premiere political art form with the mainstream arrival of Kendrick Lamar in 2012 and *Yeezus* in 2013. The former's "Alright" became an anthem for the Black Lives Matter movement, a proper protest song in a decade that became known for a resurgence in civic unrest, beginning with Occupy Wall Street and the Arab Spring. These were high-tech revolutions, ones that used Twitter to relay messages and smartphones to document injustices. The newness of it all left enough space for the public to shake things up before the powers that be could realize how democratizing these new tools truly were.

The intense energy of the time was enough to rouse D'Angelo back into the public eye. The police killings of Michael Brown and Eric Garner inspired him to finally release 2014's *Black Messiah*, a spiritual descendant to *There's a Riot Goin' On* and his first album after an almost fifteen-year absence. After a successful career as a mostly apolitical pop star, Beyoncé must have felt that she was in a strong-enough position to take a hard left turn with *Lemonade*, an album that explored her husband Jay-Z's infidelity through the lens of generational racial trauma. The lead single was "Formation," its video featuring Beyoncé standing on top of a New Orleans police cruiser in a flooded landscape that recalled the city after the devastation of Hurricane Katrina. Over a punishing Mike Will Made It trap beat, she rapped about Black pride amid a procession of African-American signifiers: a New Orleans second line parade, a Mardi Gras Indian, and, in a moment that didn't age well, a Black boy in a black hoodie resembling Trayvon Martin dancing exuberantly in front of a line of police officers.

In an outfit referencing the one worn by Michael Jackson during his legendary 1993 Super Bowl halftime show performance, Beyoncé performed "Formation" at Super Bowl 50 in 2016 with dancers dressed like Black Panthers. The choreography had the group forming the letter X on the field in a reference to Malcolm X, whom she samples on the album—his 1962 "Who Taught You to Hate Yourself?" speech. She received backlash from Rudy Giuliani on Fox News. Miami's Fraternal Order of Police threatened to boycott her upcoming show in the city. The performance had the *Los Angeles Times* asking if "Formation" was "a political call to action."

It was as much an homage to the Black Power movement as it was an aesthetic borrowing of the iconography of protest. Kendrick Lamar performed "Alright" at the 2015 BET Awards in front of defaced police cars as sparklers went off and black-clad dancers marched beside him in a performative pantomime of protest. These performances hinted at the danger, rebellious edge, and importance of what had transpired fifty years prior, remixed into sanitized protest theatre that lacked the stakes shared by those out on the front lines back then and those who were fighting injustice in the Black Lives Matter movement at the time.

Certainly, representation matters. It was powerful to see Black experience platformed on the world's biggest stages. But these performances also showed that the Black entertainers of today aren't a replacement for the Black political leaders of the '60s who were martyred while trying to improve the lives of their people. How much of Kendrick performing "Alright" dressed like an inmate on the chain gang in a mock prison at the 2016 Grammy Awards was him speaking for the disenfranchised, and how much of it was him commodifying Black struggle for a mostly white mainstream audience?

As much as artists made concrete efforts to support the movement beyond their music, their performative use of symbols to signal their personal politics has become the go-to mode of protest in the Instagram era. They were more than capable of valorizing the past but struggled to fully participate in the amorphous nature of the contemporary moment.

There's a thin line between speaking to the moment and exploiting it. Take Pepsi's 2017 "Live for Now" commercial. In the clip, Kendall Jenner, wealthy scion of the Kardashian family, interrupts her modelling photoshoot and defiantly removes her blonde wig to join a passing protest. What are they protesting? You'd never know by the signs they're holding with vague exhortations like "Join the conversation" and "Love." Jenner breaks through the ranks of her fellow protesters, and in what appeared to be a nod to the famous photograph of Ieshia Evans standing her ground while being pulled by riot police in heavy armour at a Baton Rouge protest, she hands a police officer a can of Pepsi. He cracks a knowing smirk at his fellow officers, and the conflict (?) is averted.

It was "Buy the World a Coke" for a new generation, except it was roundly panned and the ad was pulled the next day. Bernice King, daughter of MLK Jr. and Coretta Scott King, tweeted a photo of her dad being confronted by police on the front lines of a protest with the text "If only Daddy would have known about the power of #Pepsi."

One piece of sociopolitical commentary from around this time that hasn't lost any of its potency is the pitch-perfect trap satire of Childish Gambino's "This Is America." Ludwig Göransson's production melds gospel choir with a highlife-inflected guitar figure and African chants that hint at the transatlantic ties of African-American music, all without sacrificing the track's pure utility as a genuine banger.

The background ad libs from Young Thug, 21 Savage, Quavo, and more weren't just ornamental; they came across as a chorus of the dispossessed, the sound of the America that half the country feared and ignored. The song's deceptive simplicity and Donald Glover's terse, minimal lyrics added a sense of claustrophobia and coiled menace, making "This Is America" the first significant post–*Get Out* record.

The winner of Best Music Video at the 2019 Grammy Awards, the ubiquitous Hiro Murai–directed clip for "This Is America" was called "a vivid illustration of the Faustian bargain facing black America" by *Rolling Stone*, while *The Guardian* noted that Glover accurately captured "the grim surrealism of being black in America." The video launched a thousand think pieces with its hyper-referential nature, a kaleidoscopic short film that nodded at almost every corner of the African diaspora.

Rwandan-born choreographer Sherrie Silver had Gambino and a troupe of children do a variety of Black dances from around the world: the South African gwara gwara, the alkayida and azonto dances from Ghana, and Nigeria's shoki dance, as well as Black American dances like the nae nae and BlocBoy JB's "Shoot" dance. Murai and Glover urgently referenced moments of American racial strife, such as the Charleston church shooting where a white supremacist killed nine Black people, without it feeling exploitative or tasteless.

In 2017, during the height of the Me Too movement, the American public's focus shifted from racially motivated murders to sexual misconduct allegations and criminal charges against public figures such as Harvey Weinstein, Russell Simmons, Bill Cosby, and R. Kelly. The latter was met with the #MuteRKelly campaign; its organizers hoped "to end the financial support of R. Kelly's career, and help pave the way to get him convicted for sexual abuse against young women." Organizers encouraged listeners to abstain from playing his music on streaming platforms, even briefly getting his music removed from Spotify in 2018 as a result of the platform's now-defunct Hate Content and Hateful Conduct policy.

Before #MuteRKelly, the idea of boycotting a musician had mostly been the territory of American conservatives hoping to censor what they considered to be objectionable content, particularly targeting '90s rap music, controversial singers like Sinéad O'Connor, or violent movies. And while there were artists who subsequently referenced Me Too's themes in their work, such as Billie Eilish with "Your Power," Jessie Reyez's "Gatekeeper," and Kesha's album *Rainbow*, the male-dominated music industry never went through the same institutional overhaul that happened in TV and film, making it potentially less receptive to songs about these issues. After Me Too, music fans were inspired to seriously consider if they could actually separate the art from the artist.

The fever pitch of that cultural moment led directly into the Black Lives Matter protests of 2020 in the wake of George Floyd's murder at the hands of police officer Derek Chauvin. It was a "you're with us or you're against us" moment, and fans carefully observed which artists were on each side of the divide. Kendrick Lamar was criticized for not being a visible presence at the protests in the wake of his anthem

"Alright"; he eventually appeared in a dark sweatsuit with a mask covering his face at the Compton Peace Walk on June 7, 2020.

On June 2, 2020, musicians, corporations, and brands related to the music industry posted a black square on their Instagram pages, alongside hashtags like #TheShowMustBePaused, for what was known as the Blackout Tuesday campaign, spearheaded by African-American music industry marketing workers Brianna Agyemang and Jamila Thomas. Originally intended to highlight a lack of equity for Black people in the music industry, it quickly turned into an exercise in performative allyship.

Posting a black square was suddenly enough to make Starbucks feel like it had done its part for the Black community. Spotify bravely added eight minutes and forty-six seconds of silence to some of its playlists and podcasts that day "as a solemn acknowledgment for the length of time that George Floyd was suffocated." In a spectacular bit of irony, BLM activists had to urge people to stop using #BlackLivesMatter in their black square posts because they were clogging up the hashtag, thus preventing important information from getting to advocates on the ground who were actually participating in the protests. It became patently clear that the pillars of capitalism were unable to authentically reckon with this cultural moment. That they only saw it as a potential marketing win exposed the shallowness of their commitment to their customers and employees of colour.

It was this kind of absurdity that inspired me to create my most politically charged album to date, 2021's *Parallel World*. I had delved into political topics since the outset of my career, but I'd never been so direct and focused on racial inequality as I was on this release. In the wake of that album's success, I was asked to be part of a variety of panels, workshops, and discussions. I went on TV and talked about threatening to drag grocery store magnate Galen Weston by his sweater vest on my song "Nice Try."

The positive response to that album and my leveraging of social media to point out racial inequality even led me to an unexpected opportunity to work on the social media campaign for a Toronto mayoral candidate during the 2023 by-election. I toured North America with Hot Chip at the same time that I was working on this campaign, and I thought it might be interesting to merge the worlds. I invited the candidate to speak during my set at our Toronto show at History.

The candidate had a bit of a relatability issue that was exposed when I had him come onstage. There was a smattering of boos when he exhorted the crowd to vote for him. Maybe people just weren't in the mood for their synthpop party to turn into a surprise political rally. Or perhaps having an activist instead of a politician might have been more welcome. Some folks came to the merch table and thanked me for my attempt to garner civic engagement in the political process, but generally, it went on to haunt me. Most people were pissed. Folks were DMing me angrily. A stranger confronted me about it at a dinner party.

Being a socially conscious musician adds a level of seriousness to your work. Your songs stop being "(How Much Is) That Doggie in the Window." Your words can actually have an impact on the real world. This can be extremely gratifying. But with the increased pressure comes a higher level of scrutiny. Political artists open themselves up to a broader spectrum of criticism. You're no longer getting asked what your artist name means by a college radio host; now you're being tasked with giving a nuanced analysis of the Ontario provincial election on national television.

You can see why Harry Belafonte tempered his own politics after seeing first-hand the consequences of Paul Robeson's strident support of the USSR. Being a political artist can limit your prospects and potentially damage your bottom line. No one wants to get blacklisted like Sinéad O'Connor. Young artists don't want to end up pigeonholed like Phil Ochs or be subjected to a lifetime of brutality like Fela Kuti.

Today's musicians have more freedom and more avenues to reach an audience than the protest singers of the '60s did. But they are still vulnerable to censorship on platforms that they don't control. Spotify has increasingly encouraged passive, lean-back listening by prioritizing songs that aren't skipped in its algorithm. Challenging, controversial music has taken a back seat as a result, and the comparatively apolitical soundtrack of today reflects that.

While the protest singers of the past were more deeply integrated into the social movements that inspired them and thus more invested in their collective success, the artists of the social media era merely borrow the iconography of revolt to signal what they represent as individuals. An exercise in virtue signalling through identity politics, this shift has been incentivized by the same social media platforms that have left us divorced from community and cloaked in hyper-individualism. TikTok can make *you* famous, *you* can become an influencer on Instagram, and then *you* could get rich. There's room to add a little protest theatre here and there, as long as it's in a form that is acceptable to the corporate overlords.

In her 2017 *New Yorker* piece about the release of *The Legacy of Harry Belafonte: When the Colors Come Together*, Amanda Petrusich contrasts his civic engagement with that of contemporary artists. While she acknowledges that "the privatization of the listening experience and the fracturing of the monoculture has spawned a million tiny, private islands of taste," she also points out that modern musicians are seen as those who "tend to sing boldly of self-empowerment and self-growth, but rarely of collective betterment."

Nonetheless, the George Floyd protests showed that there was still a large, passionate audience of young people who care about the political leanings of brands and artists. Echoing the BDS (boycott, divest, sanction) movement against Israel that started in 2005, consumers also became more mindful on a larger scale about where their dollars were going and what exactly their spending was supporting.

The Black Lives Matter protests led to the institution of diversity, equity, and inclusion initiatives across a variety of businesses. But many disappeared soon after Trump won in 2024. The oligarchs of the tech sector signalled how they would be responding to the regime change by proudly flanking the new president at his inauguration. In 2025, Amazon, Disney, Ford, Google, Meta, Walmart, and more changed or eliminated their DEI policies.

Both Trump presidential terms have been subject to worldwide protests with massive audiences. The first day of No Kings protests attracted over five million protesters across 2,100 events around the world on June 14, 2025. The second set of No Kings protests on October 18 brought out over seven million people across 2,700 events, making it the second largest single-day protest ever after the twenty million who attended the first Earth Day demonstrations in 1970.

Director of the Center for Environment, Community, and Equity Dana Fisher told *Newsweek*, "Resistance 2.0 has taken longer to build momentum," but there have been "more protests during the first six months of Trump 2," with *FiveThirtyEight*'s G. Elliott Morris saying on his Substack that there have been three times as many protests during this term than there were at the same point during his first term.

This urge for the public to take to the streets in record numbers has not been reflected by the output of a cautious mainstream music industry. Usually a moment for musicians to use their platform to champion various causes, the 2025 Grammy Awards only had a few glancing references to politics. People looking back might be shocked to see a complete absence of support for Palestine during the broadcast. The kind of inter-genre, transatlantic, cross-racial solidarity and collective organizing we saw between Sinéad O'Connor, Public Enemy, and Vernon Reid at the 1991 Grammys feels unimaginable in today's hyper-individualistic music industry, though the 2026 Grammys did feature some anti-ICE sentiment from artists in a year where Puerto Rican superstar Bad Bunny won album of the year.

Authority figures have historically tried and failed to tamp down the public's natural inclination to dissent through art, but the protest song always bubbles back up to the surface. That's why we've seen such urgency to strike fear into the heart of any artist who dares follow in the footsteps of Kneecap and Bob Vylan through punitive efforts. The intention is to make the consequences as clear and as swift as possible: You will be investigated by the police, your shows will be cancelled, your booking agent will drop you, and your career will be over.

But young artists like Sudanese-Canadian Mustafa and Palestinian-Canadian Nemahsis are proving that being politically engaged isn't detrimental to the upward trajectory of their careers in the long run. As much as today's protest singers have learned from the missteps of the political artists before them, within the kinship of song, there remains a solidarity across generations that can't be broken.

Afterword

This book has explored so much of how music has shifted in the streaming era, but I'd like to take a moment to write about how it hasn't. Discogs sellers, app companies, social media pages, stan armies, and tech geniuses are all falling over themselves to convince us of which music is and isn't valuable. But to me, all of it is. Despite the smoke and mirrors, music is as powerful as it has always been. In our time of need, where do we inevitably turn? To the comfort of our old favourites and to the musicians who bravely speak to the times that we're in.

Part of what made the Kendrick and Drake beef so novel was how it successfully broke through the noise and gave us something to unite around, despite how toxic the circumstances were. It was one of those rare events that you had to have an opinion about, a barbershop conversation that grew legs and turned into Godzilla. These collective consciousness moments are less common in our fragmented feeds, struggling to draw the same number of eyeballs that they did back when media was more centralized.

The Golden Globes come and go without making a dent in my algorithm. But when music is the subject, the world still stops and listens like with nothing else. Taylor Swift dissed Charli xcx on her new album? I've gotta hear this. Bad Bunny is playing the Super Bowl a week after winning album of the year at the Grammys with anti-ICE protests happening outside the stadium? I'm tuning in.

It seems as if these moments move in and out of the digital news cycle with greater rapidity than ever before. The world of music is accelerating to the point that it can be difficult to keep abreast of it all. As I wrote this book, it felt as if the news held something to freshly scramble one of the essays I was writing every other day. Daniel Ek stepping down at Spotify! The constant Kneecap drama! I tried my hardest to approach the subjects in this book in a way that would stay evergreen. But of course, the only constant in life is change.

Speaking of modifications, "The Art of the Album Rollout" and "Not Like Us" were adapted from pieces that I originally wrote for my *Hazlitt* column Mind in Bloom. Parts of "A Digger's Guide" can be found in a post called "Charcuterie Music" on my *Cadence Weapon* Substack newsletter. Those two platforms functioned as my practice ground ahead of writing this book, and I highly recommend that you check out both if you're looking for additional reading.

Much of my research in making *Ways of Listening* wouldn't have been possible without archive.today. Online resources such as that and the Internet Archive that preserve elements of the old web are more important than ever in our AI-slop-ridden digital landscape.

While writing this book, I always had other artists in mind. There is a deeper utility to what I've written here for those who can apply the lessons to their own practice. Seeing the album rollout as an art form, digging for music as a meditative exercise, ignoring stat-obsessed online commentary, not being afraid to speak out against the ills of society on record: I want other musicians to remember the power that they hold within themselves and to remind them of all the things they are capable of on their own with a slight reconfiguring of their perspective.

That's what *Ways of Listening* is all about—planting my flag at the intersection of writing and music in service of doing what only I can do for those who can truly appreciate it.

Acknowledgements

Writing a book requires a level of sustained focus that outstrips any other creative discipline that I've had the pleasure of partaking in. As I get more opportunities to write, it becomes more and more clear that, despite often being a solitary experience in practice, this endeavour is truly a team effort. Shout out to everyone at McClelland & Stewart and Penguin Random House Canada. Thank you to Stephanie Sinclair for her steadfast belief in me. Thanks to my copy editor Crissy Boylan for her dedication to precision, it's always fun to get granular with you. Thanks to Hannah Karpinski for your diligent proofreading and Aruna Dahanayake for your legal advice. Thanks to Chalista Andadari, Tonia Addison, and Sabrina Papas. Big thanks to Matthew Flute for his iconic cover design.

When you find an amazing engineer as a musician, you hold onto them. In writing, the same can be said when it comes to the editing process. My most sincere thanks to my editor with the perfect surname for her profession, Haley Cullingham, for her thoughtfulness, empathy, and dedicated stewardship of my writing. Where would Mike Tyson be without his trainer Cus D'Amato? That's the vibe with us.

Thanks to my literary agent Martha Webb at CookeMcDermid for her guidance and for being a champion of my work in the writing world. Thank you to my managers Helen Britton and Griffin Elliot for keeping the machine whirring while I wrote this book and for their keen career advice. Thanks to everyone at my label Six Shooter Records and big up to my booking agent Grant Paley and everyone at Midnight Agency. Thanks to Sarah O'Driscoll for giving me permission to write about your compact disc Instagram stories.

Thanks to my family: Mick, Gena, Sierra, Alex, Massih, Anna, Indy, Julia, and the Lipscombe, Miles, Mojtehedzadeh, and Pemberton families. R.I.P. to Brett, Teddy, and Uncle Mert.

And my deepest thanks to my wife Sara for holding things down and taking care of our son while I toiled away on this book. Without her, none of this is possible. My loving appreciation for her only grows as the years go by. And big shout out to my little man Yari, who represents a generation for whom much of this book was written. If you want to learn where your passion for "doot doot" came from, you might find the reasons why in these pages.

Author photo by Vonny Lorde

ROLLIE PEMBERTON is a writer, rapper, producer, DJ, and cultural commentator who performs under the name Cadence Weapon. He won the 2021 Polaris Music Prize for his album *Parallel World*. His writing has been published in *Pitchfork*, *The Guardian*, *Wired*, *The Walrus*, and *Hazlitt*. Currently based in Toronto, Pemberton was a former Poet Laureate in his hometown of Edmonton. You can follow him @cadenceweapon on Instagram and TikTok.

https://cadenceweapon.substack.com